Creative
Garden Features

Creative
Garden Features

Roger Sweetinburgh

WARD LOCK

ACKNOWLEDGEMENTS

The publishers are grateful to the following for granting permission to reproduce the following colour photographs: Harry Smith Horticultural Photographic Collection (pp. 2, 11 (upper), 48, 54/55, 65, 76/77 and 108/109); and Photos Great Britain Picture Library (p. 11 (main photograph)). The remaining photographs were taken by Bob Challinor.

The line drawings were drawn by Roger Sweetinburgh. The coloured artwork was drawn by Mike Shoebridge.

The publishers are grateful to the following for providing locations for most of the colour photography: Geoff Ace, Merrist Wood College, Mr and Mrs J. Dean, Mr and Mrs R. Hunt and Mr and Mrs R. R. Jackson. Much of the timberwork shown in the colour photographs was constructed by B. Poplett and Son.

First published in Great Britain in 1993
by Ward Lock Limited, Villiers House, 41/47 Strand,
London WC2N 5JE, England
A Cassell Imprint

Text filmset by RGM Associates, Southport

Printed and bound in Spain
by Graficas Reunidas, s.a., Madrid

CIP data for this book is available upon application from The British Library

ISBN 0-7063-7094-5

Frontispiece: The element of surprise has always been popular in gardens, which is why this secluded fountain is especially attractive.

Contents

Preface

This book of ideas should interest anyone who is already familiar with a range of D I Y skills, especially timberwork, bricklaying and concreting, but who is looking for inspiration. It should also prove useful to landscaping contractors and to students studying various aspects of garden design and construction. The construction of most projects is described in detail with the help of diagrams and pictures. Many of the projects could be constructed in a different way to that described, and the reader is invited to modify details to suit his or her own particular needs or skills.

Ideas range from rock and water gardens to pergolas and garden buildings, from walls and paths to lighting and illusions and many other diverse projects. In many instances plants will be an integral part of the finished project, so guidance is given throughout the book on which plants to use, particularly in relation to aspect and habit.

R S

Left: Apart from the three curved pieces of wood, this gate and arch would not be difficult to construct and is ideal for framing a view.

Chapter 1

Walls

While the main purpose of this chapter is to look at specific wall projects, a number of basic principles controlling the way in which walls are built must be heeded.

Regulations

In many towns and outlying districts permission has to be sought for the construction of any type of garden wall over a certain height. This height varies from one district to another. It could be as little as 900 mm (3 ft) but is more usually applied to walls which are 1.8 m (6 ft) or more. The local authority planning officer will be able to give you details about this.

Foundations

With the exception of dry stone walls, most walls should be given a concrete foundation which is twice as wide as the wall itself. Ideally it should be set at least 75 mm (3 in) into firm subsoil and be not less than 150 mm (6 in) thick. In clay and other unstable soils, a foundation will need to be at least 225 mm (9 in) thick – often more.

Free-standing Dry Stone Walls – *(Fig. 1)*

Foundation

This is generally little more than an excavation into firm ground, lined with a bed of well-compacted stone. This leaves the wall to rely on a good snug fit between stones for much of its stability (no mortar is used).

Stone

The easiest stone to use is that which occurs naturally as flattish pieces rather than rounded boulders although, with experience and skill, these too can be used. A hard stone is best – not soft sandstone which will rapidly break up after frosts. Apart from a snug fit between stones, stability also comes from the fact that the wall will taper

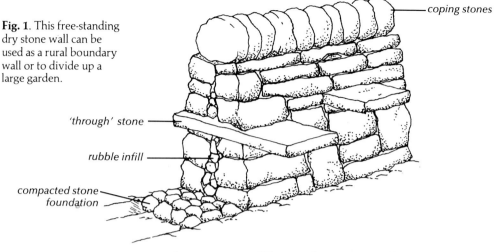

Fig. 1. This free-standing dry stone wall can be used as a rural boundary wall or to divide up a large garden.

coping stones

'through' stone

rubble infill

compacted stone foundation

towards its top – it will have a 'batter'. A wall 1.2 m (4 ft) high might have a base of 800 mm (2 ft 8 in) and taper to 400 mm (1ft 4 in) at the top. One 1.65 m (5 ft 6 in) high might be 1 m (3 ft 3 in) wide at the base, tapering to 450 mm (18 in) and so on. If you intend to build your wall along a boundary, do make sure that the whole wall is on your side.

Creating a batter

This is started by placing the first row of stones down each side of the foundation with a slight backward lean. Two parallel string lines are a useful guide here. As the wall grows in height, other string lines can be used between a pair of 'A'-shaped frames (Fig. 2) fixed at either end of the wall (but not more than 12 m (39 ft) apart, otherwise the string may sag). The shape of these frames will set the batter of the wall. A series of nails fixed down each side of the frames provides a fixing for the string lines which are moved up as the wall grows.

Fig. 2. Strings stretched between two 'A' frames will help to control the degree of batter.

Using the stone

It will be essential to shape some pieces of stone (using a pitching tool) so that they all fit tightly together. This can be minimized by carefully selecting the stone in the first place. The largest stones are usually used near the base, smaller ones near the top. With such a wide base, central voids are inevitable between the two rows of stone. These must be packed with broken stone so that the wall ends up solid from the bottom right to the top.

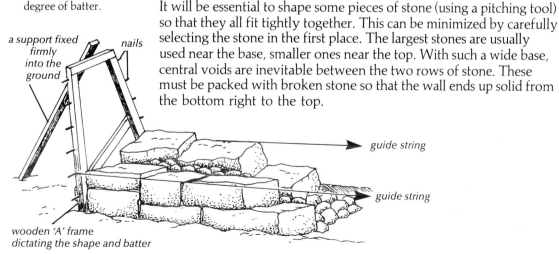

a support fixed firmly into the ground

nails

guide string

guide string

wooden 'A' frame dictating the shape and batter

It may not be possible to construct the wall in strict rows or courses. Some stones may span the equivalent of two courses (jumpers). Others will act merely as small wedges between two odd-shaped stones. The end result must be stable and 'fair-faced' – this means the outer face being as smooth as possible and not too knobbly or uneven. Additional stability can come from the occasional use of large flat stones (called 'through stones') which reach right across from one side to the other. If these can protrude sufficiently from one side, they might be used as steps up the face of the wall. Such stones can also be used as lintels over a gap which has been left as a window through the wall.

Coping

This is usually done with similarly sized stones set on edge, like books on a shelf. Never use mortar between these coping stones – it will eventually crack because a dry stone wall is designed to move with the ground. Free-standing stone walls are seldom built higher than about 1.65 m (5 ft 6 in).

Maximum height about 1.5 m (5 ft)

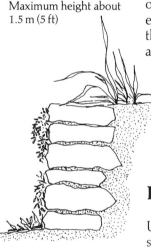

Fig. 3. This dry stone retaining wall incorporates small amounts of soil between the stones for stability and plant growth.

Right: This attractive dry stone wall shows how adaptable it can be on a slope.

Inset picture: Apart from being easy to build, a retaining dry stone wall can support a whole range of plants.

Dry Stone Retaining Wall – *(Fig. 3)*

Used for the construction of raised beds and for retaining banks of soil, these walls are relatively easy to build and can be decorated with an interesting selection of plants (see page 12).

The wall will need a batter and so the foundation should be dug out with a backward slope, preferably in firm soil. If the stone is mostly in the form of flat pieces, it can be laid in courses but as with the free-standing wall, rounded stones will make coursing difficult. As each row of stones is laid – sloping, not stepping backwards – so soil is built up firmly behind and brought thinly over the top of the stones, so that the next row can be bedded down firmly, partly with some help from soil. It is tempting to use soil to overcome all the unevenness between stones, but you should still aim for a good basic fit between stones and keep the soil to a minimum. As the wall grows, the roots of suitable plants can be incorporated so that these reach back into soil behind. When the wall nears its planned height, so courses will have to be evened up to make the top reasonably level or at least smooth. The front face of the wall can be made smoother by carefully placing a heavy piece of wood across it and banging with a club hammer. This will force any 'proud' stones into line with the rest.

Some plants suitable for dry stone retaining walls

Alyssum saxatile citrinum – silver grey leaves, yellow flowers.
Arabis – pink or white flowers.
Arenaria montana – mats of green foliage and white flowers.
Aubrieta – various colours.
Campanula carpatica – blue flowers.
Cerastium tomentosum columnae (snow-in-summer) – tight mats of silver grey foliage, white flowers.
Cheiranthus (perennial wallflower) – orange flowers.
Dianthus (pinks and carnations) – most alpine types. They prefer alkaline soils.
Geranium cinereum (alpine geranium) – mostly pinkish flowers.
Helianthemum (rock rose) – various colours.
Iberis commutata (now *I. sempervirens*) – evergreen foliage. White flowers.
Lithospermum diffusum (now *Lithodora diffusa*) – Blue flowers. Acid soil.
Lysimachia nummularia 'Aurea' – golden 'creeping Jenny'.
Papaver alpinum (alpine poppy) – raised from seed.
Phlox subulata (moss phlox) – mainly pink, mauve or white.
Polygonum vacciniifolium (now *Persicaria vacciniifolia*) – pink flowers and sometimes autumn colour.
Saxifrages – the 'encrusted' types rather than 'mossy' ones.
Scabiosa alpina (now *Cephalaria alpina*) – small, sky-blue scabious.
Sedums – most types.
Sempervivums – most types.
Thymus serpyllum (thyme) – and other 'mat' types.
Veronica prostrata – trailing mats with blue flowers.
Zauschneria californica (now *Epilobium canum*) – grey foliage and arching sprays of scarlet flowers.

Brick Walls

Here are a few variations on a brick wall. In all cases the bricks must be frost resistant (stock bricks). These walls can be given a damp proof course of engineering bricks about 150 mm (6 in) above ground level – never use a membrane in a free-standing wall.

Built to a curve

Various arrangements of bricks are shown in Fig. 4 which will result in a fairly smooth curve even down to quite a tight radius. During construction, a string must be kept anchored at the centre of the radius and a knot used as a guide for the outer edge of the curve. In addition, each brick must be lined up exactly with the centre. This can be done by having the string lined up through the centre of each brick – not down the side. If this is not done, some bricks will be twisted. Once the wall grows beyond the first few courses, it may become more difficult to use this string unless it is anchored to a rigid pole.

Fig. 4. These plans and elevations of a 225 mm (9 in) thick brick wall show how different degrees of curve can be achieved.

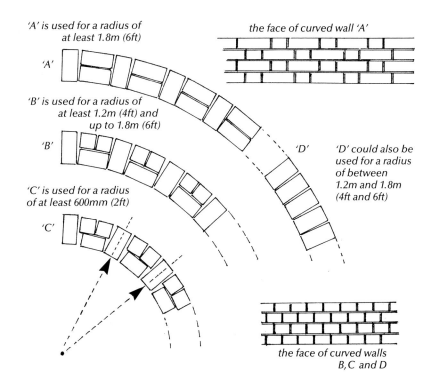

'A' is used for a radius of at least 1.8m (6ft)

'A'

the face of curved wall 'A'

'B' is used for a radius of at least 1.2m (4ft) and up to 1.8m (6ft)

'B'

'C' is used for a radius of at least 600mm (2ft)

'C'

'D'

'D' could also be used for a radius of between 1.2m and 1.8m (4ft and 6ft)

the face of curved walls B, C and D

Other styles

Fig. 5(a). Honeycomb walling with ¼ brick spaces. This wall is only 111 mm (4½ in) thick, so must have piers at least every 3 m (10 ft)
(b) A flemish bond wall 225 mm (9 in) thick with certain bricks missing to create a 'screen' effect. Piers are not so vital here.
(c) 'Raked out' joints in an otherwise flush pointed wall can be used to highlight a pattern.

A different type of brick wall could include a perforated screen as shown in Fig. 5a. Although potentially weakened by having a rather hit and miss bond, it could be made a little more stable by being slightly curved or by being given piers at either end. The wall in Fig. 5b should not be unduly weakened by the missing bricks. Brick walls can also be made more interesting by having two distinct styles of pointing which produce a contrasting pattern (Fig. 5c).

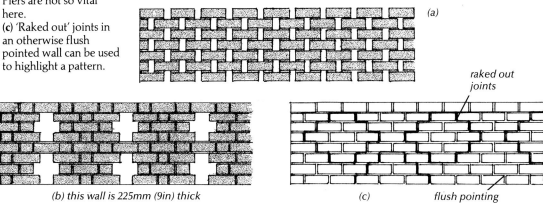

(a)

raked out joints

(b) this wall is 225mm (9in) thick

(c)   flush pointing

Three attractive examples
of stone panels
incorporated into a brick
wall.

Devonian limestone

Selected knapped flints

Jurassic limestone

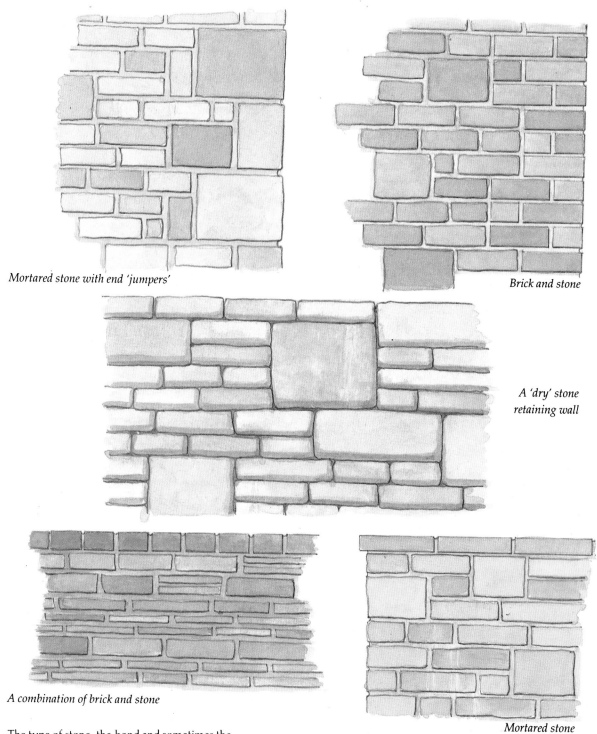

Mortared stone with end 'jumpers'

Brick and stone

*A 'dry' stone
retaining wall*

A combination of brick and stone

Mortared stone

The type of stone, the bond and sometimes the
introduction of some brickwork will help give
a wall its own special character.

Low Composite Wall – *(Fig. 6)*

Here a brick or block wall has been given a stone face in the form of 'Sussex' walling. As a free-standing wall it would be backed with brickwork, but as a retaining wall many of the bricks could be replaced with concrete blocks. Any bricks must be of stock quality with a high resistance to frost. The stone will have to be in the form of flat pieces, since space is limited. The free-standing wall begins with several courses of brickwork laid directly onto the foundation. Since a damp proof *membrane* is not recommended here, one or two rows of engineering bricks would provide an adequate barrier to rising damp. The ends and back are gradually built up, leaving an empty frame on the front. As the brickwork grows, small metal ties or pieces of expanded metal must be incorporated and left protruding from the front so that the stone-work can be properly tied in.

Fig. 6 This brick/stone wall can be built free-standing or as a retaining wall – straight or to a gentle curve.

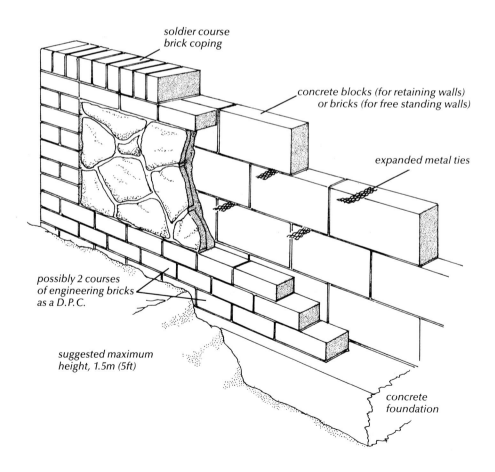

soldier course
brick coping

concrete blocks (for retaining walls)
or bricks (for free standing walls)

expanded metal ties

possibly 2 courses
of engineering bricks
as a D.P.C.

suggested maximum
height, 1.5m (5ft)

concrete
foundation

The stone-work

Once an appreciable amount of wall has been built (and has set firm) stone can be carefully selected, fitted and mortared into position, rather like vertical crazy paving. The ties must be incorporated between joints but not be allowed to protrude from the mortar, otherwise they will become rusty. Stone-work is continued along with the brick until, finally, the wall is finished off with a suitable coping – probably a soldier course of brick. There are various styles of pointing which can be used (see page 25), but for this particular type of stone-work you should avoid deeply raked-out joints. Very long walls could be given a 12 mm (½ in) wide expansion joint every 10 m (33 ft) or so (Fig. 7). A wall which is retaining a bank of soil must be given a backfill of clean stones and weepholes for the free drainage of water. Where retaining walls are to hold back a considerable weight of soil the wall thickness and size of foundation may have to be increased (see Fig. 8).

Fig. 7 Long lengths of wall should be given expansion joints every 10 m (33 ft) or so.

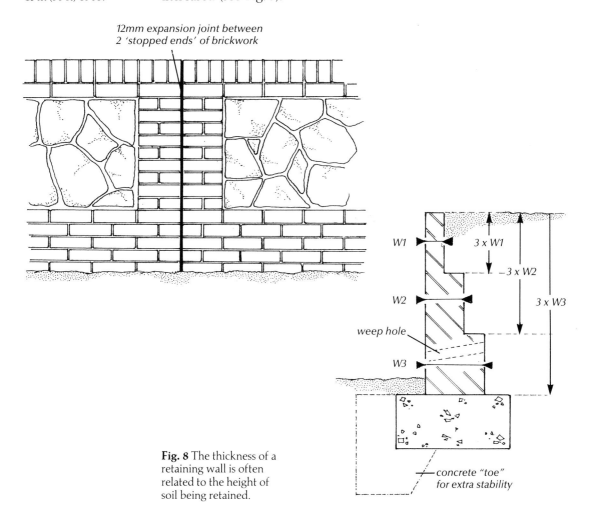

12mm expansion joint between 2 'stopped ends' of brickwork

W1   3 x W1
      – 3 x W2
W2   3 x W3

weep hole

W3

concrete "toe" for extra stability

Fig. 8 The thickness of a retaining wall is often related to the height of soil being retained.

Railway Sleeper Retaining Walls

There are two main ways of using railway sleepers to retain soil:

Horizontally – *(Fig. 9)*

Railway sleepers can be bonded like bricks in a wall with the occasional sleeper running back into the bank for extra stability. They can be given a batter which will help to prevent them from being pushed forward, or steel rods can be banged down through holes made in the sleepers into the soil below.

Fig. 9 This arrangement of railway sleepers can be used to retain up to about 1.2 m (4 ft) of soil.

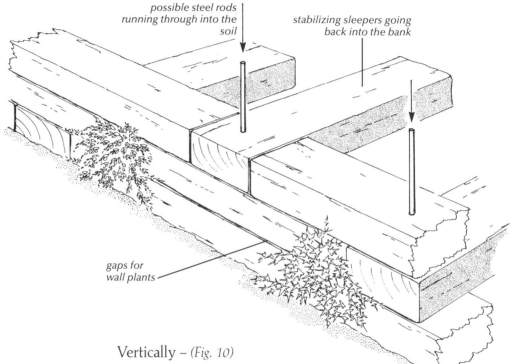

possible steel rods running through into the soil

stabilizing sleepers going back into the bank

gaps for wall plants

Vertically – *(Fig. 10)*

The sleepers may appear more decorative but can be less stable. To produce a wall 1 m (3 ft 3 in) high, at least 600 mm (24 in) of sleeper should go into the ground. Packing these around with well-compacted hardcore is better than using concrete. Concrete tends to trap water which, together with the soil, will prematurely rot the wood. A batten of tanalized timber about 100 mm × 50 mm (4 in × 2 in) should be fixed horizontally across the back of the sleepers, perhaps 150 mm (6 in) down from the top. Use long ring-shanked nails or coach screws (see page 87). For walls over 1 m (3 ft 3 in) high, try to have as much as 900 mm (3 ft) of the sleepers in the ground and perhaps use a second batten. A wall built to a concave design will display much greater strength and stability but it will then be very difficult to use battens.

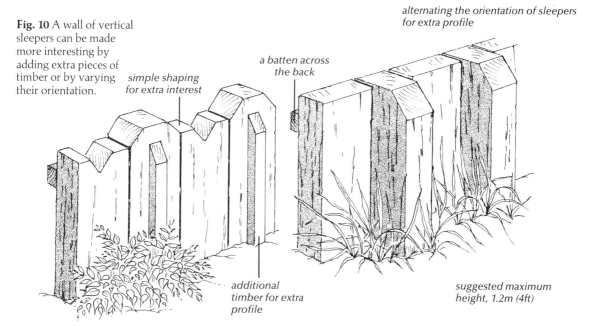

Fig. 10 A wall of vertical sleepers can be made more interesting by adding extra pieces of timber or by varying their orientation.

simple shaping for extra interest

a batten across the back

alternating the orientation of sleepers for extra profile

additional timber for extra profile

suggested maximum height, 1.2m (4ft)

'Turf' Walls

Many years ago I saw a retaining wall made from thick, upturned turves of wild heather (Fig. 11). This had been built with a batter and had grown together to produce a strong and attractive raised bed. The front was clipped with shears from time to time. The same idea could be applied to thick grass turves but only if it did not matter that grass eventually invaded all the retained soil.

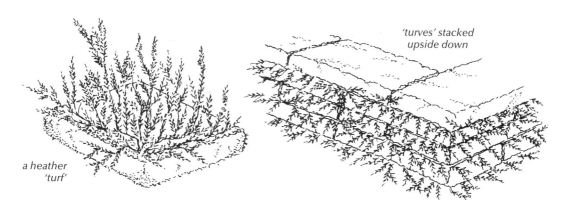

a heather 'turf'

'turves' stacked upside down

Fig. 11 Heather turves can be used to create a low, living retaining wall.

Table 1: Shrubs for walls

Shrubs	North	South	East	West	Comments	Hardy
Abelia × grandiflora		*		*	Fairly rounded habit – graceful with pink/white/purplish flowers.	semi
Acacia dealbata (mimosa)	—	*			Dislikes chalky soil. Yellow fragrant flowers. Sensitive to hard frost.	semi
Azara microphylla	*	*		*	Branches need tying back. Tiny fragrant flowers in spring.	*
Camellia	*		*	*	Needs acid soil and dislikes hot dry conditions.	*
Ceanothus – various but especially *C. × burkwoodii*, *C. dentatus*, and *C. impressus*		*		*	Can be kept trained back to a fairly neat shape. Blue flowers.	mostly
Chaenomeles (flowering quince)	*	*	*	*	Can be trained back against the wall. Pink, red or white flowers in early spring.	*
Chimonanthus praecox (winter sweet)		*		*	Not easy to train neatly against the wall. Fragrant cream-coloured flowers in winter and early spring.	*
Cotoneaster horizontalis	*	*	*	*	Grows naturally tight against a wall.	*
Cotoneaster simonsii	*	*	*	*	Can be trained to grow fairly flat against a wall.	*
Cytisus battandieri		*		(*)	Large, three-lobed leaves and large yellow, pineapple-shaped flowers. Needs tying back to a wall.	semi

    Ceanothus   *Chaenomeles*   *Cytisus*

Shrubs	North	South	East	West	Comments	Hardy
Escallonia – all types	(*)	*		*	Grows well against a wall but has an arching or untidy habit.	usually
Euonymus japonicus – variegated forms	*	*	*	*	Can be kept fairly tight up against a wall with pruning. Especially useful on a north-facing wall.	*
Ficus carica (fig)		*		*	Needs initial training back against the wall.	*
Forsythia suspensa	*	*	*	*	Sparse but large yellow spring flowers. Needs tying onto wires and can be untidy.	*
Fremontodendron californicum		*			Attractive bold foliage, large saucer-shaped yellow flowers. Can be vigorous and needs plenty of space.	semi
Fruit – includes apples, pears, peaches, nectarines, plums, cherries etc.		*		*	Usually trained on wires as cordons, espaliers or fans.	*
Garrya elliptica	*		*	*	Conspicuous green catkins during the winter. Can be kept fairly neat but needs plenty of space.	*
Magnolia grandiflora		*		*	Large, glossy evergreen leaves and, eventually, creamy white flowers. Needs plenty of space.	*
Pyracantha (firethorn) – all types	*	*	*	*	Can be kept very neat and quite tight against a wall. Especially useful on a north-facing wall.	*

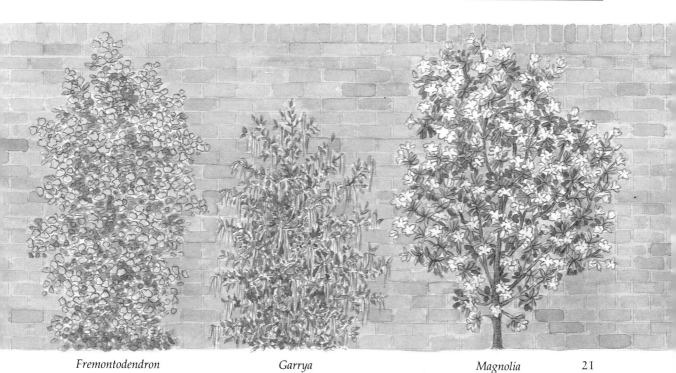

Fremontodendron   *Garrya*   *Magnolia*   21

Table 2: Some climbing plants for garden walls

Plants	North	South	East	West	Hardy	Self Clinging	Wires
Actinidia kolomikta (Kolomikta vine) – pink-tipped leaves		*			semi	stems	*
Aristolochia macrophylla (Dutchman's pipe)		*		*	semi	twining stems	*
Campsis grandiflora (Trumpet vine)		*		*	semi	stems	*
Clematis – various types. Roots must be in shade	*some	*		*	*	leaf stalks	*
Eccremocarpus scaber – orange flowers		*		*	semi	tendrils	*
Hedera – ivy (various)	*	(*)	*	*	mostly	suckers	
Humulus lupulus aureus (golden hop)	*	*	*	*	*	twining stems	*
Hydrangea petiolaris (climbing hydrangea)	*		(*)	*	*	suckers	
Jasminum nudiflorum (winter jasmine)	*	*		*	*	stems	*
Jasminum officinale (common white jasmine) and *J. × stephanense*		*		*	semi	stems	*
Lonicera (honeysuckle)	*	*	*	*	*	twining stems	*
Parthenocissus (Virginia creeper)	*	*	*	*	*	suckers	

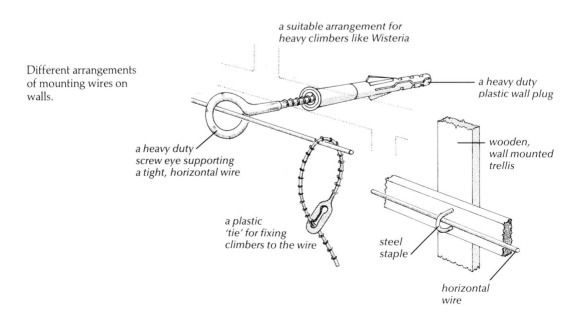

Different arrangements of mounting wires on walls.

a suitable arrangement for heavy climbers like Wisteria

a heavy duty plastic wall plug

a heavy duty screw eye supporting a tight, horizontal wire

a plastic 'tie' for fixing climbers to the wire

wooden, wall mounted trellis

steel staple

horizontal wire

Plants	Aspect				Hardy	Self Clinging	Wires
	North	South	East	West			
Passiflora caerulea (common passion flower)		*		*	semi	tendrils	*
Polygonum baldschuanicum (now *Fallopia baldschuanica*) (Russian vine)	*	*	*	*	*	twining stems	*
Roses – see separate section below	*	*	*	*	*	stems	*
Solanum crispum 'Glasnevin' and *S. jasminoides* (jasmine nightshade)		*		*	semi	stems	*
Trachelospermum jasminoides		*			semi	self clinging	(*)
Vitis coignetiae	(*)	*		*	(*)	tendrils	*
Vitis vinifera 'Purpurea' (purple vine)		*		*	(*)	tendrils	*
Wisteria floribunda 'Macrobotrys' (now *W.f.* 'Multijuga') and *W. sinensis*		*		*	*	twining stems	*

CLIMBING ROSES Some cultivars are successful on east and north-facing walls:

Yellow – 'Golden Showers'; 'Gloire de Dijon'; 'Maigold';
Pink – 'Madame Grégoire Staechelin';
Red/vermillion – 'Danse du feu'; 'Etoile de Holland'; 'Guinée';
White – 'Madame Alfred Carrière'.

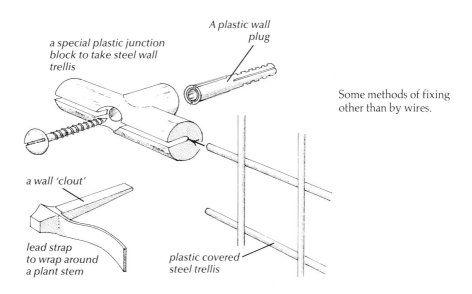

a special plastic junction block to take steel wall trellis

A plastic wall plug

a wall 'clout'

lead strap to wrap around a plant stem

plastic covered steel trellis

Some methods of fixing other than by wires.

Chapter 2

Patios and Barbecues

Patio Design

Fig. 12 A wide range of
patterns in brick paving
can be enhanced by the
use of more than one
colour.

The following projects show some different ways of using paving and
of shaping patios. From the vast selection of manufactured slabs and
blocks there is always the opportunity to produce interesting patterns
using various colours and/or a mix of sizes (Figs. 12 and 13). It is often
possible to mix different makes of product where sizes and perhaps
textures are compatible. The colour and style of pointing can also
have a dramatic effect on the overall appearance (Fig. 14).

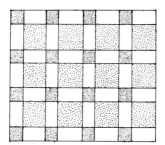

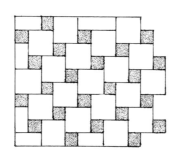

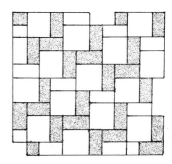

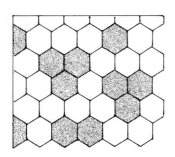

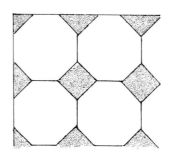

*combinations of paving slabs
incorporating different colours*

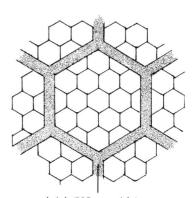

*brick (225mm wide)
running through 450mm
hexagonal slabs*

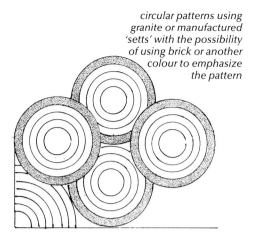

circular patterns using granite or manufactured 'setts' with the possibility of using brick or another colour to emphasize the pattern

Fig. 13(a) A 'fleur de lys' pattern using setts, with a second colour to pick out the pattern.

(b) Different arrangements of block paviors using two colours.

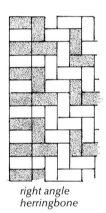

right angle herringbone

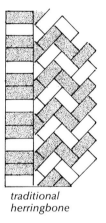

traditional herringbone

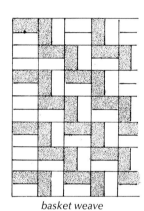

basket weave

Fig. 14 Various styles of pointing which can be applied to joints in paving or walling.

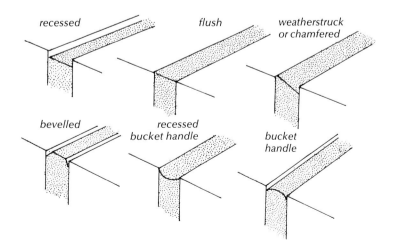

recessed

flush

weatherstruck or chamfered

bevelled

recessed bucket handle

bucket handle

Foundations

All patios (with the exception of timber decking) must have extensive foundations. Ideally, all soft topsoil should be removed and any 'making up' done with clean hardcore or scalpings (crushed stone). Where very thin paving units are being used – particularly ceramic, terracotta and concrete tiles – a smooth concrete slab foundation is best.

Fall

All paved surfaces (except timber decking) must be given a slope or a 'fall' – usually of about 1 centimetre per metre and preferably away from any adjacent building. If this is not done, water is likely to collect on some patios unless suitable drains are incorporated. Sometimes water can be encouraged to simply drain away into adjacent borders.

Patio Project 1 – *(Fig. 15)*

This patio does not fit against a house but could go anywhere in the garden to catch the sun. It is at ground level so there will not be any steps and rainwater will be able to drain off into the surrounding borders (and away from the raised bed).

Paving

Its overall shape means it would be difficult to construct with square or rectangular slabs because of all the cutting needed. Bricks or block paviors could be used in a circular pattern but difficulties would occur near the centre as the circle tightened. Small, concrete block setts specifically designed for circular patterns are ideal and so too is crazy paving. Other possibilities include exposed aggregate concrete with its pebbly surface or just shingle (see pp. 51–52). All these materials either need or look more attractive with some form of edging, possibly brick (or block paviors). Do use hard, stock bricks for all paving projects.

Raised bed

This might be built in brick or stone to a height of 400 mm (1 ft 4 in). Its walls should be at least 225 mm (9 in) thick, probably comprising an inner skin of concrete blocks and an outer skin and coping of the decorative material (such as that illustrated on page 16). Seclusion around the back of the patio is achieved with creeper-covered trellis, and an arch might be incorporated which could lead to another part of the garden.

Pool

This would be constructed either from a butyl liner which has been pre-welded to shape, or from concrete blocks (225 mm or 9 in thick) set on a concrete base and rendered. If blocks are used do not forget to finish these low enough, so that there is room for poolside paving over the top.

Planting

Fig. 15 This secluded patio can be built in a sunny spot away from the house.

Fragrant or aromatic plants/herbs are a good choice for a patio, particularly for the raised bed. Either side, against the fences, taller shrubby plants can provide relatively maintenance-free screening, whereas lower planting would be needed around the pool so that the water and the rest of the garden are not obscured.

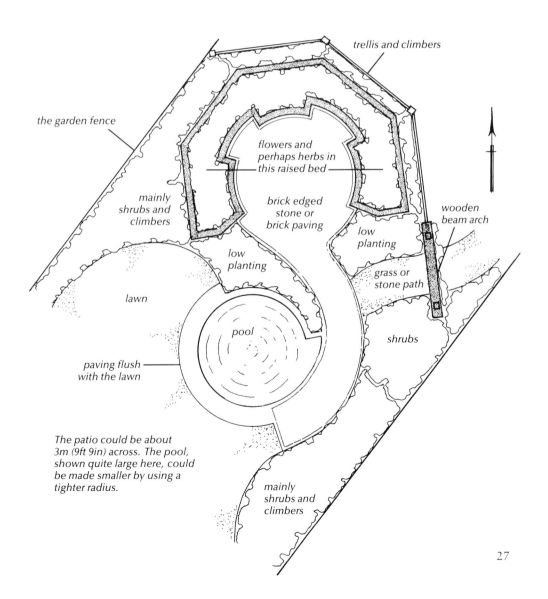

trellis and climbers

the garden fence

flowers and perhaps herbs in this raised bed

mainly shrubs and climbers

brick edged stone or brick paving

wooden beam arch

low planting

low planting

grass or stone path

lawn

pool

shrubs

paving flush with the lawn

The patio could be about 3m (9ft 9in) across. The pool, shown quite large here, could be made smaller by using a tighter radius.

mainly shrubs and climbers

Patio Project 2 – *(Fig. 16)*

This design can also be placed out in the garden to catch the sun and not against the house. Since it is larger than the previous example, there is room for a pergola to provide some shade, and space too for a garden table and chairs for outdoor eating.

Paving

Most of the angles are 45° or 90°, making this project ideal for various types of paving. Herringbone brickwork would fit particularly well without excessive cutting. Square or rectangular slabs also fit the sort of shapes used here with most of the cutting being simple 45° diagonals. Perhaps the only paving which might prove very difficult and somewhat unsatisfactory is hexagonal slabs.

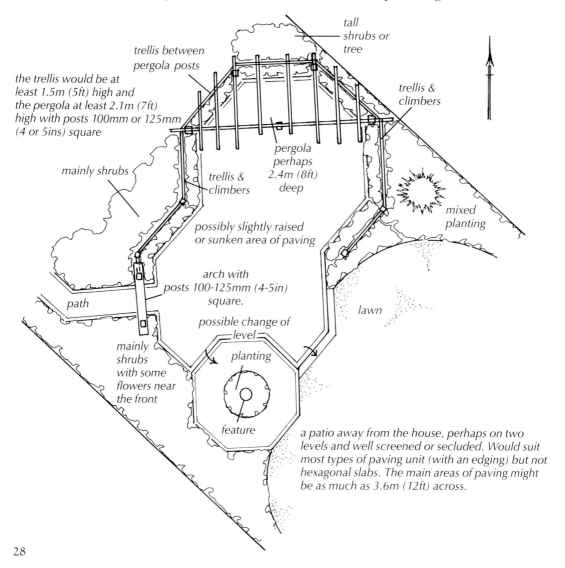

tall shrubs or tree

trellis between pergola posts

the trellis would be at least 1.5m (5ft) high and the pergola at least 2.1m (7ft) high with posts 100mm or 125mm (4 or 5ins) square

trellis & climbers

mainly shrubs

trellis & climbers

pergola perhaps 2.4m (8ft) deep

mixed planting

possibly slightly raised or sunken area of paving

arch with posts 100-125mm (4-5in) square.

path

lawn

possible change of level

mainly shrubs with some flowers near the front

planting

feature

a patio away from the house, perhaps on two levels and well screened or secluded. Would suit most types of paving unit (with an edging) but not hexagonal slabs. The main areas of paving might be as much as 3.6m (12ft) across.

Fig. 16(Opposite) This patio would also be built away from the house and is large enough for outdoor dining and entertaining.

Levels

There is the suggestion that this patio could be sunken. If this is the case, special attention must be paid to surface water drainage. As a raised patio, it would require a step down onto the lawn, the lower tread being made flush with the grass for easy mowing. There is also the opportunity to have a small octagonal area at a different level to the rest. Here a feature like a sundial, bird bath or even a small pool and fountain could be introduced to add extra interest. With these changes of level and their inevitable steps comes the need to choose a material which can be used both as a general edging and as a step. Bricks or perhaps brick paviors are a better choice than concrete block paviors since the latter often have a bevelled edge and would therefore be unsuitable for the step risers.

Fig. 17(a) While different levels and angles make the patio interesting, there is plenty of planting to soften the edges.

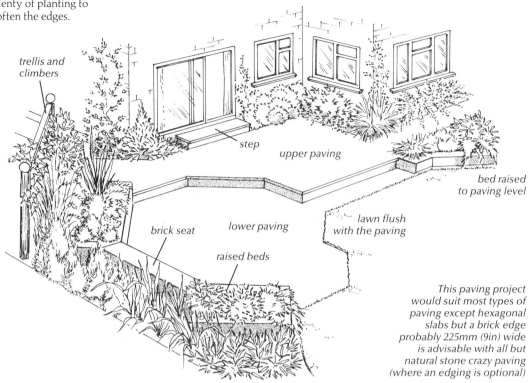

trellis and climbers

step

upper paving

bed raised to paving level

brick seat

lower paving

lawn flush with the paving

raised beds

This paving project would suit most types of paving except hexagonal slabs but a brick edge probably 225mm (9in) wide is advisable with all but natural stone crazy paving (where an edging is optional)

Patio Project 3 – *(Fig. 17)*

This third patio adopts a similar angular shape but takes advantage of a sunny house corner. Here the ground is low in relation to the house (and its door sills) so has been built up to produce a split level patio. Paving should always, however, be kept at least two brick courses or 150 mm (6 in) below the house damp proof course.

Paving

With similar shapes to the previous patio, similar materials can be used but again, because of cutting, an edging of some sort will be needed, especially along the edge of steps. Bricks are the ideal choice because the use of these can be extended into the construction of the raised beds and seat. If natural stone crazy paving is used, however, no edging would be needed and the steps and beds could also be built in a matching stone. (The seat could also be built from slatted timber instead of brick or stone.)

Raised beds

For the construction of raised beds, no matter how small these may be, it is always advisable to use a strip foundation – not a solid raft – so that the central area can remain free from concrete and be free draining. The raised bed foundations here must be kept as low in the ground as possible so that there is ample room to bring the paving material right over the top and up to the walls.

Planting

Around the house there are beds for wall planting. Never make these less than 450 mm (18 in) wide otherwise, with the house foundations close by, the soil in a narrower bed could dry out too quickly. There is space too for planting against boundary fences which, combined with planting in the raised beds will provide a pleasant setting for a spacious and interesting patio.

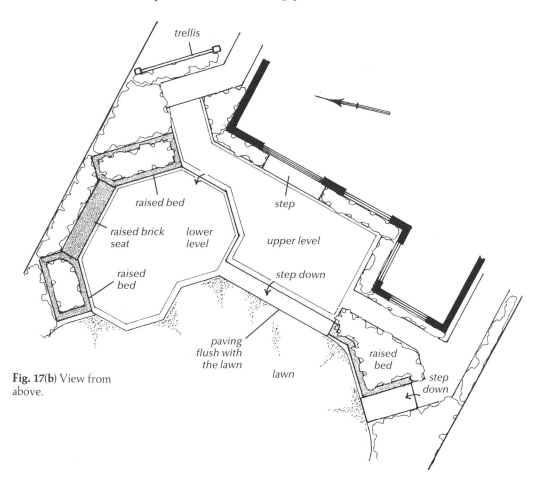

Fig. 17(b) View from above.

trellis

raised bed

step

raised brick seat

lower level

upper level

raised bed

step down

paving flush with the lawn

lawn

raised bed

step down

Patio Project 4: Timber Decking – *(Fig. 18)*

This timber-decking patio will need a basic framework of sawn timber joists measuring perhaps 50 mm × 150 mm (2 in × 6 in). These will have to be supported on short brick or concrete columns (at least 300 mm × 300 mm or 1 ft square) with a damp proof membrane immediately beneath the timber. This basic frame (with its subsequent cross members and decking) should be heavy enough never to move on these brick columns but it could be bolted down if necessary. Slightly thinner joists are fixed between these main ones at about 375 mm (15 in) centres in order to support the decking, which is usually made from planks 100–150 mm (4–6 in) wide and 15–20 mm (¾ in) thick. A gap of about 1 cm (⅜ in) must be left between planks so that water can always drain away quickly. Ideally these planks

Fig. 18(a) A patio of timber decking produces a completely different atmosphere to one of paving and is often easier to construct.

gravel path

timber steps up

The height of the decking above ground will depend upon the height of the door sill. In this example, it is about 450mm (18in)

should be planed timber (as opposed to the rougher and more splintery 'sawn' type), while planks of hardwood are better still, though far more costly. The main uprights for the balustrading will have to be bolted securely to the main frame so that, when complete, the balustrading can resist considerable stress. Here again, planed timber or even hardwood is better than sawn timber. The steps are constructed from the same materials and the whole project stained or treated with a non-toxic product (not creosote).

As a raised balcony-type feature it offers a unique opportunity to look down on the planting, so plenty of border space has been left all around the decking for plants such as dwarf bamboos, grasses and other foliage plants which will retain some foliage during the winter. A feature like this may be built around the main house entrance, in which case lighting would be particularly appropriate.

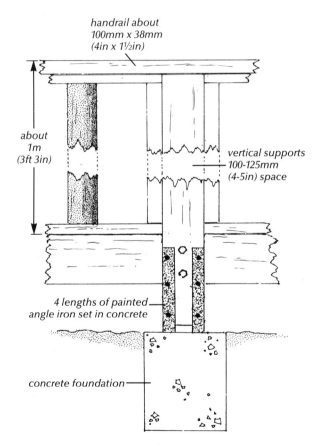

Fig. 18(b) Details of construction of balustrade and decking.

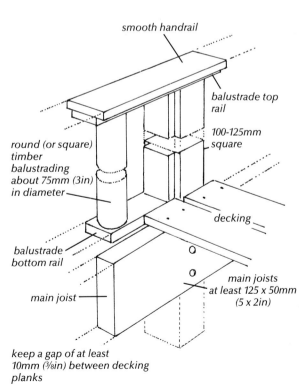

Table 3: Plants for a shady patio – borders, tubs or pots

Plant	Comments	Hardy
Arundinaria (bamboo), especially *A. viridi-astriata* (now *Pleioblastus auricomus*)	Probably best in border soil rather than pots.	*
Astilbe cultivars	Best in damp shady borders (herbaceous).	*
Aucuba japonica (spotted laurel) cultivars	Decorative, variegated foliage and easy to grow, but may grow quite large.	mostly
Buxus sempervirens (common box) (now *B.s.* 'Aureo-variegata') and *B.s.* 'Aurea'	Both are ideal for tubs and pots. They can be clipped into different shapes. Good in dry soil.	*
Camellia cultivars	Need acid soil. Do not allow them to dry out.	*
Choisya ternata 'Sundance'	Best in border soil rather than in pots/tubs. Grown for its attractive evergreen golden foliage.	mostly
Convallaria majalis (lily of the valley)	Seems to tolerate most conditions including dry soil. Grown for its white fragrant flowers.	*
Epimedium perralderianum	A ground-cover plant with dainty leaves which prefers acid soil.	*
Euonymus fortunei cultivars *E. japonicus* cultivars	All grown for their attractive, often variegated foliage. *E. japonicus* grows quite tall but *E. fortunei* is low growing and spreads.	*
Euphorbias – various	Many are grown for their attractive, often evergreen foliage, others for their greenish-yellow flowers and bracts. Herbaceous.	*
Filipendula ulmaria 'Aurea'	Beautiful golden ferny foliage. Herbaceous.	*
Geranium 'Johnson's Blue' and others	Easy to grow herbaceous plants which should flower under most conditions, including dry soil.	*
Hebe cultivars – many different types	Those with coloured foliage are probably the most successful in shade. Evergreen.	mostly
Hedera helix cultivars and others	All reliable in shade and dry soil with a wide range of variegation and leaf shape to choose from.	* (not *Hedera canariensis*)
Helleborus cultivars (Christmas and lenten roses)	Virtually evergreen herbaceous plants often with attractive foliage but grown mainly for their pink, reddish, white or green flowers.	*
Hosta cultivars	Many different types of colourful foliage to choose from. They prefer damp soil. Herbaceous.	*
Ilex cultivars (holly)	Ideal for large tubs or for spacious borders. *Ilex crenata* 'Golden Gem' is quite dwarf.	*
Iris foetidissima	Although it has attractive evergeen foliage, it is grown mainly for its conspicuous orange seeds.	*
Kalmia latifolia (calico bush, mountain laurel)	A neat but eventually quite large evergreen shrub with unique pink flowers. Prefers damp, acid soil.	*
Lamium maculatum 'Beacon Silver'	An evergreen creeping plant with striking silver foliage which sometimes turns pink.	*
Laurus nobilis (sweet bay)	Makes a good specimen plant for a pot or tub but may suffer in heavy frost.	semi
Mahonia × media 'Charity'	In open soil, this is a large vigorous plant but is less so in a large tub. Attractive foliage and fragrant yellow flowers. Evergreen.	*
Omphalodes verna (blue-eyed Mary)	Grown mainly for its blue flowers in the spring. Herbaceous.	*
Ophiopogon planiscapus nigrescens	An unusual 'grass-like' plant with black strap-shaped, evergreen leaves. Not tall.	*

Plant	Comments	Hardy
Pernettya mucronata	Plant several to be sure of berries which can be pink, red or white. Prefers acid soil and not too dry.	*
Pieris floribunda 'Forest Flame' *P. japonica* 'Variegata'	Both ideal for large pots or tubs of moist acid soil. Young shoots will be damaged by frost.	*
Polygonatum multiflorum (also *P. × hybridum*) (Solomon's seal)	A curious arching herbaceous plant with small white flowers.	*
Pulmonaria angustifolia	Especially valuable in early spring for its pink and blue flowers. Herbaceous.	*
Rodgersia pinnata elegans	A herbaceous plant with leaves which resemble those of *Aesculus* (horse chestnut).	*
Rhododendrons and azaleas	All grow well in tubs or large pots of moist acid soil. Do not allow to dry out.	*
Senecio 'Sunshine' (formerly *S. laxifolius*, now Brachyglottis 'Sunshine')	Probably better in borders than in pots or tubs. Attractive silver foliage and yellow flowers. (Evergreen).	*
Spiraea × bumalda 'Gold Flame' and 'Gold Mound' (also *S. japonica* 'Goldflame' and 'Gold Mound')	Both attractive, deciduous shrubs with golden foliage.	*
Stranvaesia davidiana (also *Photinia davidiana*) 'Palette'	An evergreen shrub with attractively variegated leaves in pink, white, green and some red. It will need some pruning to keep it bushy.	
Trachystemon orientalis	A herbaceous plant with large leaves and small blue flowers in early spring.	*
Viburnum davidii	An evergreen shrub with attractive foliage. May eventually outgrow a tub since it is not particularly easy to prune.	*
Viola labradorica	A violet with deep purple leaves and blue flowers. Prefers not to be dust dry.	*
Vinca cultivars (periwinkle)	All grow well in shade and dry soil. *Vinca major* may prove too vigorous for some situations. *Vinca minor* has smaller leaves and is less vigorous. Evergreen ground cover.	*

Table 4:   Plants for a sunny patio – borders, tubs or pots

Plant	Comments	Hardy
Herbs and aromatic plants, including:		
Artemisia 'Powis Castle'	Silver, ferny foliage.	*
Helichrysum lanatum (now *H. thianschanicum*) (curry plant)	Silver/grey foliage.	*
Lavandula angustifolia 'Hidcote' and others	Lavender.	*
Lippia citriodora (now *Aloysia triphylla*)	Lemon scented foliage – not very hardy.	semi
Origanum vulgare aureum	Small plant with golden aromatic foliage.	*
Rosmarinus officinalis	Rosemary.	semi
Ruta graveolens 'Jackman's Blue'	Blue foliage with a strange smell. May produce an allergy.	*
Salvia officinalis	Sage – forms available with purple or variegated foliage.	*

Plant	Comments	Hardy
Santolina chamaecyparissus	Silver-leaved cotton lavender.	*
Thymus – various forms	Thyme – both shrubby and carpeting types.	*
Other plants:		
Callistemon (bottle brush)	Fuzzy pink flowers along the stems which look like bottle brushes.	semi
Ceratostigma willmottianum	Small, rather loose shrub with blue flowers.	mostly
Cistus crispus cultivars	Low-spreading evergreen shrub with mainly pink flowers.	mostly
Convolvulus cneorum	Not bindweed but a small, beautiful silver-leaved shrub.	semi
Cordyline australis	A palm-like plant with green (or purple) grassy leaves. Not entirely hardy. Looks good with bedding plants.	semi
Eucalyptus gunnii	Could be grown as a clipped or regularly pruned bush which will develop small, rounded blue/grey leaves.	semi
× *Fatshedera lizei*	Attractive glossy evergreen foliage but needs a wall or corner to lean up against.	semi
Fuchsia cultivars	Only some are hardy. Others will have to be overwintered indoors. Good in tubs.	semi
Heather – *Erica* and *Calluna*	These provide colour for both summer and winter in the form of flowers and foliage. Some need acid soil.	*
Helianthemum cultivars (rock rose)	A wide range of flower colours available. They do not grow very large but are tolerant of hot sunny situations.	*
Magnolia stellata 'Rosea'	Potentially quite a large shrub but will grow well in a large tub of preferably acid soil. Must not be allowed to dry out.	*
Myrtus communis (myrtle)	A neat evergreen shrub with white flowers in late summer, ideal for a large pot or tub. A variegated form is available.	semi
Phlomis fruticosa	Grey/green leaves and distinctive yellow flowers. Will tolerate hot dry conditions.	*
Phormium (New Zealand flax)	Attractively coloured or variegated strap-shaped leaves makes this an ideal specimen for the centre of a tub in association with bedding plants or heathers.	semi
Punica granatum (pomegranate)	Potentially a large shrub but can be grown in a tub for its interesting scarlet flowers. Needs a long hot summer for any fruits to ripen.	semi
Rhododendrons and azaleas	Can be grown in large tubs of acid soil on a sunny patio as long as they are kept moist and are never allowed to dry out.	*
Roses – various	There are many dwarf or 'patio' roses available which can be grown in large pots or tubs of soil which is heavy rather than full of humus. Do not allow them to dry out.	*
Strawberries	Ideal for pots and tubs but do not allow them to dry out.	*

Note: **Many** climbing plants can be grown in large tubs if no borders are available. It must be remembered that these plants should **never** be without moisture and food. Their vigour will always be limited by the volume of soil and amount of food and water they receive.

Barbecue – *(Fig. 19)*

Built-in barbecues can be very simple or highly elaborate. The materials which are used for the actual fire must be both heat and frost resistant, so stock or engineering bricks are far superior to ordinary house 'flettons'. Concrete products are usually quite resilient as are the harder types of walling, but soft sandstone and poor quality concrete products should both be avoided.

 The most basic requirements are for a tray on which to build a fire and an adjustable grill for the food. The fire tray can either be a perforated sheet of steel or closely spaced bars, remembering that

Fig. 19(a) A purpose-built barbecue area including a work surface, cupboards and fixed seating.

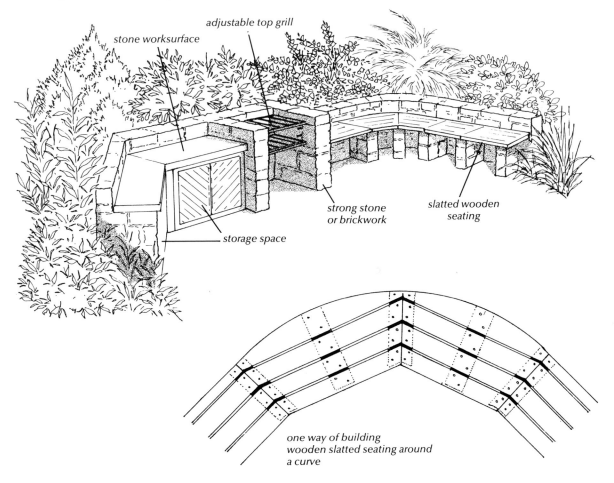

stone worksurface

adjustable top grill

strong stone or brickwork

slatted wooden seating

storage space

one way of building wooden slatted seating around a curve

Dimensions: The work surface could be any length but, along with the actual barbecue, should be about 500-600mm (20-24in) deep and up to a comfortable working height. The seat, which could extend to any length, would be about 400mm (16in) high and 350-400mm (14-16in) deep. The width of the barbecue should be at least 500mm (20in) – more if used by large groups of people.

lumps of charcoal are the most widely used type of fuel. The food grill must be adjustable so that the food can be raised or lowered above the heat source. Although both the fire and the food grill are normally built up to a comfortable working height, some of the simple 'camping' type barbecues are formed from a pit in the ground. If gas is being used instead of charcoal, it can either be built into some sort of structure or be used in conjunction with a fully portable barbecue. Apart from these very basic requirements there are many ancillary pieces of equipment and structures which can be introduced to make the barbecue quite elaborate and a fully fitted centre of activity.

Fig. 19(b) A barbecue's fire tray can be of closely set bars or, as here, a tray of steel. Above it, flanges provide adjustable heights for the grill.

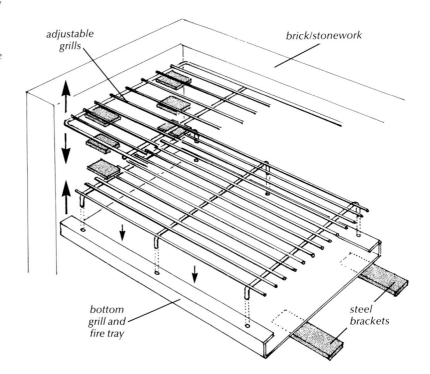

Additional Facilities

WORKSURFACES next to the barbecue are always useful – made from slabs of stone, concrete or perhaps slatted wood.

STORAGE CUPBOARDS can easily be built under work surfaces for crockery, cutlery and even the temporary storage of food.

SEATS can either be in the form of wooden slats fixed down onto plinths or walls, or as free-standing picnic benches arranged on an adjacent area of paving or patio. Seats can usually double as low worktops.

PAVED AREA AND PATHS   If the barbecue is not on or next to an existing patio, it will need some sort of paved surface even if this is only shingle. A good, smooth path (smooth enough for trolleys of food) is always helpful as well, linking the house with the barbecue area.

LIGHTING   is important for evening barbecues but does often attract unwelcome insects, so ultraviolet insect traps can be hung around just outside the barbecue area to entice the bugs away. Lighting will need a properly installed electricity supply. For different types of lighting, see Chapter 9.

PLANTING   around the general area will obviously enhance its appearance and atmosphere both day and night. Raised beds are a particularly good way of introducing plants since the walls can be made into low seats.

For some people, having barbecues is more than just casual weekend fun. It can become a regular part of an outdoor lifestyle with all sorts of additional embellishments, including some sort of roof.

ROOF   This is often made from a transparent material (see Chapter 8), sometimes with a thin cane or lath 'ceiling' which will partially hide the roofing materials but still let some light through. Alternatively, a 'solid' roof can be used, perhaps pine panelled on the underside and with some form of lighting.

COOKER HOOD AND FLUE   Once a roof has been built over a barbecue, a hood and flue are usually necessary. These can be built from aluminium, stainless steel or copper.
   Alternatively, a proper brick or stone chimney can be built to incorporate the barbecue, its cupboards and so on. A chimney may, in fact, inhibit the action of the fire and need the addition of a fan to produce a forced draught.

WATER   Once the outdoor barbecue starts to become an 'indoor' affair a sink with at least cold running water could be added.

ELECTRICITY   Power sockets (all-weather type) are always useful, particularly for things like electric carving knives, coffee percolators, hand mixers, kettle and even a small fridge.
   Other refinements could include a speaker system for piped music, a bar for serving drinks, telephone and so on.
   All barbecues are smoky and smelly, so whatever type of barbecue is built it should be positioned away from any houses. Barbecues can also become unsightly, covered in soot and fat. Some careful planning and positioning may be needed to ensure that this is not visible from the house.

Chapter 3

Steps

There are three main aspects to steps:

(*i*) style
(*ii*) proportions and dimensions
(*iii*) construction.

Style and construction are demonstrated in the following projects but some explanation is needed on how to calculate the size of tread and height of riser. Firstly the total height and the total horizontal distance which the steps are to span must be carefully measured. In many cases, the materials from which the steps are to be made will have already been chosen.

Calculating the riser

A reasonable height for a riser is between 150–200 mm (6–8 in). Some of the chosen materials will have to be pieced together (including some mortar) to produce a riser which falls somewhere within this range. The total height to be spanned can now be divided by the height of one riser in order to calculate approximately how many risers will be needed. It is unlikely to work out exactly. If there are a number of millimetres left over (spare), which represent less than half of a riser, these could be shared out equally between all the risers, increasing their height slightly. This can usually be achieved by increasing the thickness of mortar joints, although these should never exceed 12 mm (½ in). If, on the other hand, the number of millimetres left over amount to more than half a riser, all the others could be robbed of a few millimetres so that there are enough available to turn this 'part' riser into a whole one. The height of these risers will obviously be slightly smaller than at first predicted. Once again, these adjustments could be made using the layers of mortar but a mortar joint should never be less than, say, 7 mm (¼ in).

Calculating the tread

Once the number of risers (and therefore steps) has been decided, the total, horizontal distance to be spanned can be divided by this number so that the size of each tread can be calculated.

Oversail

Below: Here is an example of steps, raised beds and paving designed and built around 90° and 45° angles.

A tread is often extended over the edge of a riser in order to produce an 'oversail' which will cast a small shadow and give each step extra definition. This oversail need not, at this stage, be included in any calculations.

Fall

All steps should be given a slight fall (forwards) to shed water. This can be achieved by tapping down the front edge of a tread as soon as it has been laid. It is, therefore, important to have this top mortar joint at least 7 mm (¼ in) thick so that this 'fall' adjustment can be made. This process does not affect the overall calculations since it will not alter the overall height of the steps.

Where a simple flight of steps is to be fitted into a smooth bank so that soil (and probably plants) just spill over the end of each tread, it is better to begin at the bottom with a tread and not a riser. This has the effect of pushing the whole flight into the bank a little way but it will result in extra excavation. An extra tread will probably be needed right at the top but this does not change the calculation because each riser, including the top one, does already contain the thickness of a tread.

Each of the following three projects would start with a foundation for the bottom (first) riser. This should be concrete set down into firm ground. A good foundation is particularly important for steps since a lot of use occurs in a relatively small area. Once the first foundation is in and the riser built up to the desired height, any soft soil must be removed from behind and the area (which will be underneath the first tread) built up with hardcore, scalpings and/or concrete to just below the top edge of the riser. The first tread can then be laid, perhaps with an oversail. The next riser is built on top of this firm foundation before the area behind is, once again, thoroughly prepared for the second tread... and so on.

Do not forget to build a slight forward fall into each tread so that rain can flow away and not 'puddle'.

Fig. 20(a) Steps with various aspects coming off an area of paving or patio.

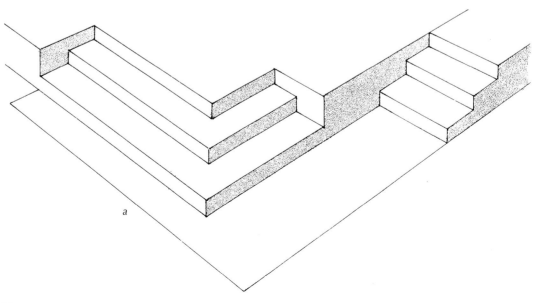

a

Corner Steps

The steps illustrated in Fig. 20a feature an external corner and could be built in almost any paving material, although an oversail may be difficult to achieve in bricks or paviors. Difficulties may also arise if square slabs are used because it is not easy to keep the pattern going in both directions and have an oversail without cutting some slabs, especially near a corner. One way of achieving this without any cutting is shown in Fig. 20b. The risers are, in effect, set back inside the tread by the same amount as the overhang or oversail. In practice, this means that a narrow fillip of mortar, perhaps tinted to match the slabs, is needed all along the back of the slabs on each tread. This will maintain the slab pattern in both directions (see plan view in Fig. 20c) as well as avoid cutting. None of these problems occur with crazy paving nor with brick paving (so long as it is used without any oversail). At least some of the materials used in the construction of the steps should match those in the wall. Where slabs are used, perhaps risers could be in the same material as the wall.

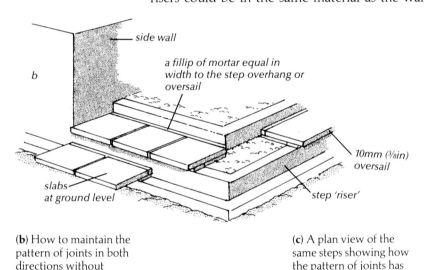

side wall

a fillip of mortar equal in width to the step overhang or oversail

b

10mm (⅜in) oversail

slabs at ground level

step 'riser'

(**b**) How to maintain the pattern of joints in both directions without having to cut any slabs.

(**c**) A plan view of the same steps showing how the pattern of joints has been maintained.

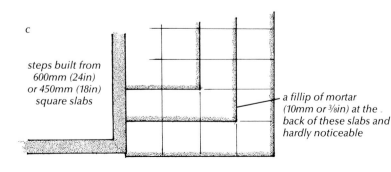

c

steps built from 600mm (24in) or 450mm (18in) square slabs

a fillip of mortar (10mm or ⅜in) at the back of these slabs and hardly noticeable

Previous page: This modern front garden layout shows how effective curved steps can be when built from 'stock' bricks.

Bevelled Steps – *(Fig. 21a)*

Bevelled steps would not be suitable for slabs if these had to be given a cut edge around the angled corner – it would look unsightly. It might, however, be possible to arrange cut slabs so that the cut edges did not end up on the bevelled or angled corner, but this would depend on the size of slabs being used. Larger ones might be available from which a special shape could be cut. These steps could be built from bricks but careful arranging and cutting would again be needed on the angled corner (Fig. 21b), and the depth of tread will have to be decided in relation to the size of a brick so that cutting can be kept to a minimum.

An ideal material for these steps is natural stone both for the treads and the risers, possibly in conjunction with stone walls. Raked out pointing would enhance the stone.

Fig. 21(a) Steps with angled or bevelled corners can be built from a wide range of materials.

(b) When built in brick, these steps would have no oversail and would need some careful cutting around the bevelled corners.

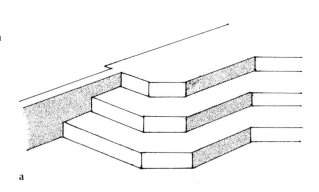

a

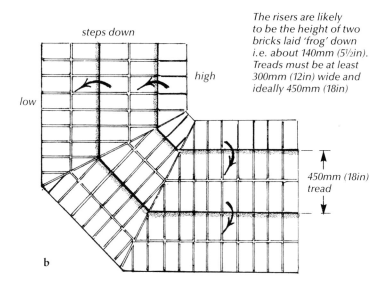

steps down

high

low

The risers are likely to be the height of two bricks laid 'frog' down i.e. about 140mm (5½in). Treads must be at least 300mm (12in) wide and ideally 450mm (18in)

450mm (18in) tread

b

The Circular Steps – *(Fig. 22)*

Circular steps make a pleasant change from angular ones. The risers are only about 105 mm (4 in) high because the radius edging bricks have been used on their side in order to keep the joints as tight as possible. At the top, the circle is too small to have the same brick edging so bricks have been cut in half and placed cut end down, producing a riser of the same height. The smallest practical radius using the full bricks is about 1 m (3 ft 3 in). Anything smaller than this will produce unacceptably wide joints. The small radius used for the top step should not be less than about 600 mm (2 ft). Pointing around the edge of each riser will have to be done particularly carefully and neatly since the joints are widest at this point.

The treads can be filled with all manner of decorative materials, from miniature brick or concrete setts, to granite setts, pebbles set in concrete or even exposed aggregate concrete. A particularly effective combination would be broken stone paving within the brick edging used in conjunction with the brick and stone walling shown earlier in Fig. 6 (see page 16). The extra row of bricks part way around the top circle help to provide an opportunity for the flower borders to link in neatly.

Good circles and radii can be achieved using a string anchored firmly in the centre (see page 13).

Fig. 22 These curved steps can easily be built into an existing corner and incorporate a wide choice of materials.

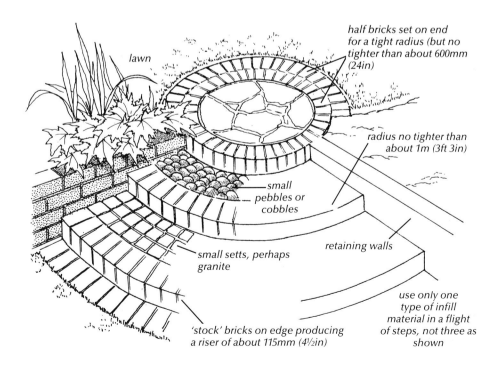

lawn

half bricks set on end for a tight radius (but no tighter than about 600mm (24in)

radius no tighter than about 1m (3ft 3in)

small pebbles or cobbles

small setts, perhaps granite

retaining walls

'stock' bricks on edge producing a riser of about 115mm (4½in)

use only one type of infill material in a flight of steps, not three as shown

Chapter 4

Garden Paths

Quite apart from any aesthetic considerations, all paths must be functional, so careful design is essential.

Width

In busy areas of the garden (particularly to and from the house) a path should be at least 900 mm (3 ft) wide. In other parts of the garden, where use is only occasional, a width of 600 mm (2 ft) is usually sufficient.

Route

A busy path should take a reasonably direct route. If this is not possible then some planting or some other feature here and there may deter people from taking short cuts across a lawn. Where use is entirely leisurely, then a winding and more devious route will add charm and interest.

Edgings

Since paths usually pass through areas of lawn and alongside flower borders, an edging of some sort is often needed to prevent lawn edges from breaking down and border soil from invading the path. In addition, many path materials are loose and need containing. There are a number of different edgings illustrated on the following pages (Figs. 23 and 24).

Drainage

Left: A hoggin/shingle path can look attractive in almost any setting but is especially suited to a country or cottage garden.

Water may collect and persist on some paths which have been edged. This is most likely to occur where the path runs across level ground, where non-porous materials have been used or in heavy clay soil. Water can at least be drained to the sides if the path is given a camber. Having breaks in the edging might also help while wider, busier paths could be given a system of drains and gullies placed in strategic positions. The fall or camber can then be manipulated to take advantage of these.

Hoggin/Shingle Path – *(Fig. 23)*

This example shows two types of edging: timber and brick.

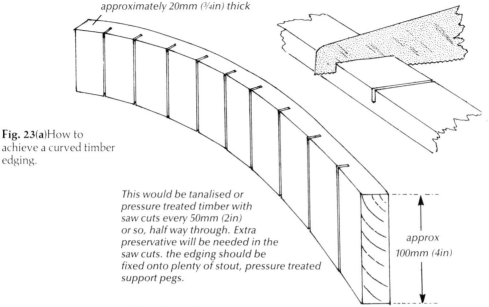

approximately 20mm (¾in) thick

Fig. 23(a) How to achieve a curved timber edging.

This would be tanalised or pressure treated timber with saw cuts every 50mm (2in) or so, half way through. Extra preservative will be needed in the saw cuts. the edging should be fixed onto plenty of stout, pressure treated support pegs.

approx 100mm (4in)

Timber edging

This is ideal against a lawn because it will eventually become virtually invisible yet keep a firm, well-defined edge to both the path and the grass. Only pressure treated timber is used. Long strips about 20 mm (¾ in) thick and 100 mm (4 in) wide (deep) are fixed to stout wooden pegs (38 mm × 38 mm or 1 ½ in square), which must go as deep as possible into the ground on the lawn side. Where timber edging has to go around steep curves, it can be cut half way through every 50 mm (2 in) or so and bent so that the cuts are closed up. All these cuts must be treated with extra wood preservative. Ideally, if the grass is already well established about 300 mm (12 in) should be peeled back in the form of turves and the timber edging installed so that the turves can be rolled back over the top of it. The path will obviously have to be excavated before these edgings are put in, down to reasonably firm soil. If this is quite deep, say 300 mm (12 in), some of the space will have to be built back up with hardcore, well consolidated. If this depth is much less, scalpings would probably be better (again, well consolidated). The surface of the path must finish about 25 mm (1 in) down from the top of the edging. The hoggin will go on top of the hardcore to a compacted depth of between 50–75 mm (2–3 in) so the hardcore (or scalpings) itself should come more or less level with the bottom of the timber after compaction. The timber edging in Fig. 23b is both relatively inexpensive and easy to install. It will also be long lasting if it and especially any saw cuts are throughly treated with preservative. A timber edging is ideal alongside a lawn where a mower can ride, unhindered, over the top. The edgings shown in Fig. 24b are also easy to install but are unsuitable for a lawn edge. Instead, they should be used to separate the path material from a flower border.

Brick edging

On the opposite side, the excavation can be widened and the hardcore extended so that the (stock) brick edging benefits from the compacted base material. The brick edging is mortared into position so that its top is more or less at the same height as the timber edging.

The hoggin

This is a natural mixture of stones, sand and a little clay. Once all the edgings are in place and have set firm it is raked out evenly, perhaps with a fall or camber so that it is about 20 mm (¾ in) down from the top of the edgings. A vibrating plate is better for compacting hoggin in a path than a roller. The hoggin must not be dusty dry nor saturated and you should avoid working in the rain. As the plate passes up and down, so the hoggin will compact. Before making the final passes, a skim of shingle (pebble size 10 mm or less) can be spread and vibrated into the surface. Finally another skim of shingle can be used to dress the compacted surface. It is very important to rake the hoggin exactly to the desired levels before vibrating, since the plate cannot be relied upon to even out bumps and dips.

Fig. 23(b) A country garden path using traditional materials. It can be straight or curved.

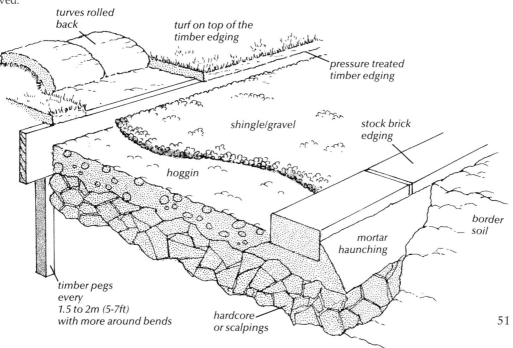

turves rolled back

turf on top of the timber edging

pressure treated timber edging

shingle/gravel

stock brick edging

hoggin

border soil

mortar haunching

timber pegs every 1.5 to 2m (5-7ft) with more around bends

hardcore or scalpings

51

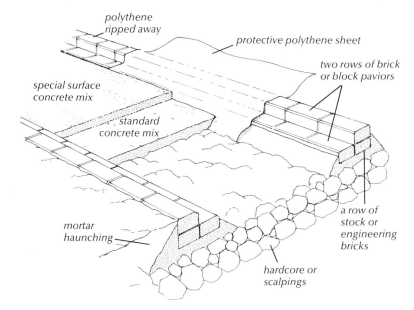

two rows of brick or block paviors

polythene ripped away

protective polythene sheet

special surface concrete mix

standard concrete mix

mortar haunching

a row of stock or engineering bricks

hardcore or scalpings

Fig. 24(a) This modern exposed aggregate concrete path with its block or brick edging can be given a very attractive modern surface.

Modern Block and Exposed Aggregate Path – *(Fig. 24)*

(b) These alternative path edgings are ideal alongside a border but not the lawn – they hinder mowing.

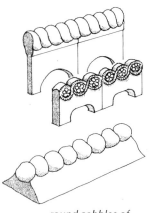

round cobbles of a selected size set in mortar

The excavation and foundation for this path would be similar to that described for the hoggin path (see page 51). Assuming that the aggregate used is a brown or yellowish colour, both edges would be brown or buff-coloured concrete block paviors. If the path is to finish below ground level two rows of blocks are used down either side but only one row if the path is flush with the ground. The blocks are mortared down each side, onto the bed of hardcore (or scalpings), leaving the space between for concreting. Because concreting will be messy, thin polythene must be draped over all the edging and down onto the hardcore for protection.

Concreting

The main batch of concrete can be a 'normal' mix of cement and all-in-ballast (1:6). It is laid and tamped between the edges so that it finishes about 25 mm (1 in) down from the top of the edging blocks. A 'special' mix is then made incorporating a high proportion of 10 mm shingle or some other attractive aggregate. If the chosen aggregate does not resemble the 'normal' all-in-ballast then instead of ballast, use sand with the aggregate, along with the cement. This special mix is laid over the previous batch so that it finishes flush with the blocks. After about five hours (depending on temperature) the surface can be very gently washed and brushed clean to expose the aggregate. Use a *soft* brush. A polythene sheet should then be placed over the whole job so that the concrete can set hard. After a few days, this is removed and the thin protective polythene torn or blow-torched away. The exposed aggregate may still have a cement 'bloom' partially masking its true colour. This can be cleaned off using a proprietary (acid) stone cleaner.

Do not ignore the problem of drainage when planning this path because it is completely non-porous.

Chapter 5

Water Garden Projects

All the projects described here assume that naturally occurring water is not available. They are, therefore, all contrived and rely upon various materials to provide a watertight structure. Apart from bricks, blocks, stone etc, the two materials most frequently referred to are butyl and concrete.

Butyl

This is an extremely tough, flexible man-made 'rubber' sheet or membrane which comes in several thicknesses. Virtually any size of sheet can be created by welding pieces together and for very large projects – lakes for example – this welding would be carried out on site. Welding can also be used to create unusual shapes for special situations where no visible folds or creases are wanted. The life of butyl is reputed to be in excess of 25 years and is not affected by sunlight (unlike plastics and PVC). Butyl is normally black but other colours or effects may be available from time to time. As with other similar liners, it should be given an underlay to protect it from sharp objects. This underlay, a geotechnic membrane, is a felt-like woven fabric which is often white or grey, but it should not, of course, be visible beneath the liner. The underlay would be particularly important in stony ground.

ESTIMATING THE SIZE OF SHEET   This can be done using the following, simple formula:

total length = twice the maximum depth + length + sufficient overlap at either end.

total width = twice the maximum depth + width + sufficient overlap at either side.

Butyl can easily be cut with a sharp knife or scissors, but is only really welded successfully by using special equipment. It is possible to repair small holes and slits with a puncture repair kit (including a vulcanizing fluid) similar to that commonly used to repair tyre inner tubes. Materials which have similar properties to butyl may require a different technique for repair, so refer to the manufacturer's recommendations.

Concrete

A mix of 1 part of cement to 6 parts of all-in-ballast will be strong enough for most projects. A 'stiff' mix produces the strongest concrete and will stack easily up fairly steep sides, but is likely to have more voids running through it than a wetter mix (through which water can escape). Concrete is not normally completely watertight and needs additional treatment to make it so. Its strength can be significantly enhanced by the inclusion of steel reinforcing. This must not be too near the surface – at least the equivalent of two stones (from the ballast) beneath the surface – otherwise it could eventually rust and weaken the concrete.

WATERPROOFING   A wet mix with a 'fatty' surface is likely to be the most watertight, at least from a structural point of view, with few visible voids on the surface, although it will not be possible to stack it up the sides of an excavation. With this wetter type of concrete, final waterproofing might be achieved by simply adding a waterproofing agent (powder or liquid) to the wet mix. An alternative would be to spray or paint the hardened surface with silicone, resin or a water-proofing 'paint'. Most silicones and resins are colourless. Resins are the most durable (and expensive) while silicone needs renewing from time to time. Resins usually comprise of two agents which are mixed together and applied with a paint brush. Silicone is more usually applied with a sprayer which must be washed out immediately after-wards, otherwise the nozzle will block up. Sealant paints are available in various colours but, again, may need renovating every few years.

Another, quite different product, is a substance called sodium silicate. It is colourless and dissolves in water. When painted onto the surface of concrete it combines with the calcium of the cement to produce a hard surface glaze. A side benefit of this is that all the free calcium is locked up and cannot migrate into the water to harm pond life.

The voids which tend to occur in the surface of stiffer concrete mixes where there is no fattiness to seal them over may not be sealed sufficiently with resin or silicone and certainly not with sodium silicate. Some of the thicker paints might succeed with several coats.

RENDERING   A more successful approach would be to 'render' the surface of this 'stiffer' concrete. Rendering is a mix of sharp or washed sand and cement in the following proportions:

1 part of cement to 5 parts of sand
perhaps with the addition of an appropriate waterproofer.

A fairly soft mix is needed. The easiest way to apply rendering is to brush it on and work it in with a stiff hand brush or soft-medium broom head. Two applications are usual. The first will go into any voids and perhaps end up 5 mm or so thick. A second layer will add another 5–10 mm or so. An alternative is to 'trowel' or 'float' it on but again as two coats. It is important to apply it to 'green' or freshly set concrete which is still damp on the surface, and to prevent each application from drying out quickly by covering with polythene. If a waterproofer is not added to the mix, something could be sprayed or painted onto the surface, just to make absolutely sure, although the rendering itself should be watertight. If the basic concrete mix has had a waterproofer added, it may be difficult for the rendering mix to stick to the surface unless there are plenty of voids or scoring marks for it to key into. When using concrete, always try to incorporate *two* methods of waterproofing, just in case.

Water Pumps

All those projects based on moving water will need a pump. There are two basic types: *surface* and *submersible*.

SURFACE PUMP   This pump operates *out* of water. It must be housed in a dry, ventilated chamber as close to the lowest part of the water feature as possible and, ideally, a little lower than the water's surface. This is to ensure that the pump remains full of water when it is switched off. It will need two pipes, one from the lowest area of water into the pump and the other from the pump to the highest point, from where the water is to cascade. In addition, a safe electricity supply is needed.

Surface pumps tend to be used for the largest projects where a very high volume of water has to be moved.

SUBMERSIBLE PUMP   This type of pump is situated *in* the water at the lowest end of the system. It does not, therefore, need a special chamber or an intake pipe. It sucks water directly into itself, but does need a pipe to deliver water to the top of the system. Once again, an electricity supply will be needed. An extra deep section of water in the lowest part of the system will help to conceal the pump although the majority are quite compact.

Submersible pumps are ideal for most domestic projects including fountains, even where quite a high volume of water is needed, and are easier to install than a surface pump.

ASSESSING THE SIZE OF PUMP   Where a project relies heavily on a certain effect being created with moving water, it is crucial to have sufficient power available. Most pumps are calibrated in gallons or litres per hour. As all pumps have to work against gravity, the higher the water has to go, the lower the volume of water moved. This height to which the water will have to be lifted is called the 'head'.

Another limiting factor is friction inside the delivery pipe – a long length will reduce the volume of water delivered. Dirt may also gather around the intake, despite a filter, and restrict the flow still further.

To have some idea of what a certain flow per hour looks like, take a bucket or container of a known capacity, say 5 litres, 1 gallon or whatever, place it under a bath tap (or similar high volume tap) and find out how long it takes to fill the bucket at a certain flow. By doing some simple arithmetic you will be able to calculate the flow per hour. If that particular amount of water is too little or too much for the effect you are trying to achieve, alter the flow and re-calibrate. It will then be possible to study a performance table and, taking into account 'head', length of pipe etc, find several makes of pump that can easily deliver the required flow. This will be the very minimum acceptable performance.

On all but the very smallest water features, it is always wise to select a pump which can produce a significantly better flow than is needed because its efficiency is likely to drop. A control valve can then be put in line so that the flow may be increased or decreased as necessary. A similar comparison can be drawn with a hi-fi amplifier. It is much better to have an amplifier more powerful than is needed and use it at half volume than to run an underpowered device flat out all the time.

Electricity supply

Since most pumps are fitted with only a relatively short length of cable, an 'all-weather' exterior socket will have to be mounted quite close by. Ideally, it should be on a short, stout, wooden post and positioned as much out of sight as possible. A pair of sockets is useful in case another feature, such as underwater lighting, is wanted. An armoured cable should link sockets back to the house and connect with a fused, earthed spur with a safety trip switch. The fuse must have a suitable rating and all electrical work should be carried out by a qualified electrician.

If a transformer is being used in conjunction with a lower voltage pump, this must be housed in a dry ventilated chamber as close to the pump as possible. If it is installed a long way from the pump there could well be a significant loss of voltage and a disappointing flow of water.

Pond overflows

In many cases, where the pond is a 'natural' feature out in the garden, away from the house and with plenty of planting space around, an overflow is not really necessary. Where the water feature might look silly with water flooding over surrounding paving a simple overflow can be arranged so that water will fill to just below the brim but no higher. This must, however, be linked to a suitable outfall, for example a soakaway.

Water filters

There are many filters on the market which are both efficient and economical to run. Most 'formal' water features including ponds containing fish, and features which rely on clear water would benefit from the installation of a filter.

Planting

'Natural' water features containing a wide range of aquatic and marginal plants will often keep clear by a natural biological process and may not need a filter. A reduction in algae and a good biological balance will be helped by some of the following aquatic plants.

Aquatic plants

Aponogeton distachyum – has leaves which float on the surface.
Azolla caroliniana – a small floating fern to cover the surface.
Ceratophyllum demersum (hornwort) – an oxygenating weed which floats freely beneath the surface.
Eichhornia crassipes (water hyacinth) – a floating plant with blue flowers but is not entirely hardy.
Elodea canadensis (Canadian pondweed) – useful for oxygenating.
Fontinalis antipyretica (willow moss) – forms dense, dark green mossy thickets under water and oxygenates.
Hottonia palustris (water violet) – useful for oxygenating.
Hydrocharis morsus ranae (frogbit) – leaves look like miniature water lily leaves and are therefore useful for covering the surface. Small white flowers.
Lagarosiphon major – one of the most useful oxygenating plants.
Lemna (duckweed) – various types. All useful for covering the surface but can often become invasive.
Myriophyllum verticillatum – an oxygenating plant with rich green, underwater foliage.
Nymphaea (water lily) – useful for covering the surface. Var. 'Pygmaea' is ideal for small ponds.
Potamogeton crispus – green or slightly bronze foliage, useful for oxygenating.
Tillaea recurva – a small-leaved plant for deep or shallow water and for oxygenating.

Those plants which do not float free in the water will need planting into soil. Apart from the natural or 'nature' pond where this soil is provided, baskets or containers filled with a heavy loam can be used and placed at an appropriate depth beneath the surface. A stone mulch will help to prevent the loam from rising and clouding the water.

The Natural or 'Nature' Pond – *(Fig. 25)*

This project uses a butyl liner together with a geotechnic underfelt. It also requires tanalized timber or bull-nosed concrete edging strips with concrete haunching. This specification is ideal for ponds between, say, 6 m (20 ft) and 50 m (162 ft) across but could be modified for smaller ponds.

Excavation

It is vital to create the correct shape of excavation. The top third to one half of the pool's circumference will comprise of a fairly shallow, gently sloping shelf. The central area will be deeper with this depth being created by a much steeper slope (about 45°). The upper, shallow part will be backfilled with about 150 mm (6 in) of good soil on top of the liner, so the excavation should begin *vertically* around the edge about 150 mm (6 in) deep, then slope gently down from there until it reaches the steeper part. The depth in the centre will depend, to some extent, on the size of the pool but it could be as little as 450 mm (18 in) in the smaller pools but as much as 1.5 m (5 ft) in larger pools. This will obviously influence the type of pondlife which develops.

During excavation the best and most stone-free soil is put on one side in readiness for backfilling, and the surface of the finished excavation should be firm, smooth and as stone free as possible. Butyl is tough but can be torn by a stony surface.

Inner edge

Once excavation is complete an upstanding edge of timber or concrete is constructed just back from the edge of the steep slope. This upstand should be about 150 mm (6 in) high and will help contain the soil backfilled in the shallow part of the pond. A timber strip would be nailed to firm pegs and all rough edges removed, or bull-nosed concrete kerbs would be concreted and haunched in position with all concrete being left perfectly smooth.

Spreading the liner

The geotechnic underfelt is then spread evenly over the whole excavation followed by the sheet of butyl with any creases being evenly distributed. Extra underfelt or butyl offcuts could be placed over the upstanding edgings beneath the main sheet for additional protection from chaffing. The lower, central part of the pond can then be partially filled with water to weight down the liner, which is encouraged to follow *loosely* the contours of the upstanding edging, before coming across the shallow area and finally ending up vertical around the outer edge of the excavation.

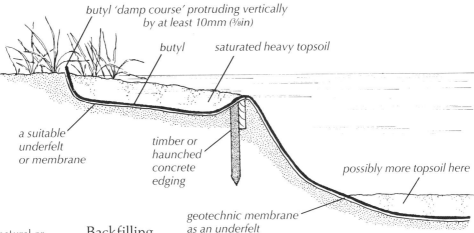

butyl 'damp course' protruding vertically
by at least 10mm (⅜in)

butyl   saturated heavy topsoil

a suitable
underfelt
or membrane

timber or
haunched
concrete
edging

possibly more topsoil here

geotechnic membrane
as an underfelt

Fig. 25 A natural or 'nature' pond with shallow water around the edges enabling small creatures to move in and out with ease.

Backfilling

The best soil is then carefully backfilled on top of the liner in this upper, shallow area, being compacted at frequent intervals and ending up level with the surrounding garden soil, and up to the top of the upstanding kerb/edging. The pond can then slowly be filled right up to the outer edge before excess butyl is trimmed off. It is, however, *vital* to leave about 10 mm (⅜ in) of butyl protruding vertically all the way round (with firmed soil on each side). This must be left to prevent water from the pool being sucked out into the surrounding garden. Eventually plants or marginal weeds will grow on either side of this and hide it.

Water levels

If the pool has been constructed in level ground, water will lap evenly all around the top edge but if the ground slopes, the water will be one-sided leaving a muddy 'beach' on the high side. This will not matter since it will soon be covered with planting of some sort. The liner is unlikely to be visible or be damaged since it is beneath at least 150 mm (6 in) of soil. During droughts, the water level will drop but unless the shallow portion of the pool is exceptionally shallow and does not slope down much towards the centre, the soil in this area should still remain covered with water. Only if the water level drops below the top of the inner kerb/edging will the butyl become visible. Little maintenance is necessary but the growth of plants within the 'beach' areas will be copious. The pond may need topping up from time to time.

High water table

Problems can arise if the area has a high water table. If this rises above the bottom level of the pond, the central area of butyl may rise to the surface. If it is predicted that this could happen, a heavy layer of good soil can be placed on top of the liner during construction. If this problem occurs after the pond has been finished, heavy weights like concrete blocks wrapped in black polythene or butyl will have to be carefully lowered down into this deep part of the pool so that the liner is pushed back into position.

Rock Pools and Cascade – *(Figs. 26 and 27)*

Design

This is a project which obviously benefits from a sloping site. Ideally, it should be positioned away from large trees where leaves and roots can be a problem. Although only two cascades or waterfalls are shown here, the slope may be such that several waterfalls are possible. It helps to measure the total drop available from one end of the area to the other in order to plan the number and height of falls. The sound which water makes tumbling down into a deep section of water will be completely different to that cascading into shallow water. The design should produce falls of different heights to provide some interesting variations.

The basic structure will be steel-reinforced concrete which is certainly not flexible, so the ground into which it is being built must be firm and stable, not recently made up. In theory there is no limit to the size of a project like this but the design should avoid long narrow sections (usually in the form of streams) since these are vulnerable to cracking. The whole system should be broad-based and compact, not long and drawn out.

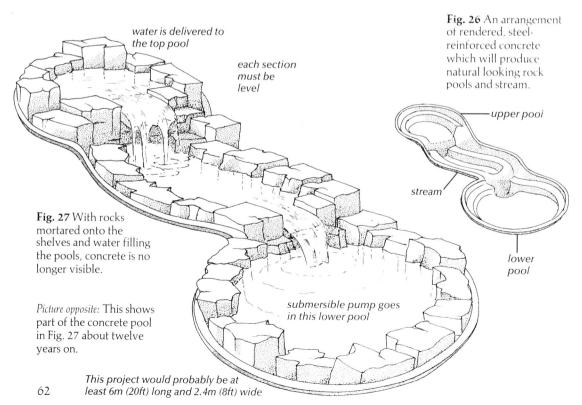

water is delivered to the top pool

each section must be level

Fig. 26 An arrangement of rendered, steel-reinforced concrete which will produce natural looking rock pools and stream.

upper pool

stream

lower pool

Fig. 27 With rocks mortared onto the shelves and water filling the pools, concrete is no longer visible.

Picture opposite: This shows part of the concrete pool in Fig. 27 about twelve years on.

submersible pump goes in this lower pool

This project would probably be at least 6m (20ft) long and 2.4m (8ft) wide

Construction – concreting

The pools and streams will all be 'free form' which means that the concrete (and steel) is used to line mainly bowl-shaped excavations. Sides cannot, therefore, be vertical. If vertical sides are wanted, concrete block walls will have to be built onto a raft-shaped base and, for this type of project, that is less satisfactory. Excavations have to be generous, particularly in width since, in order to create a natural-looking feature, quite a lot of stone will have to be mortared onto the *inside* of the concrete pools, and still leave a reasonable area for water. Ideally, the whole system should be cast in one operation with steel bars 5–10 mm ($\frac{3}{16}$–$\frac{3}{8}$ in) thick being used, wherever possible, approximately midway through the concrete. The concrete should be about 150–200 mm (6–8 in) thick.

It is quite important to create perfectly level pools and level streams. If a stream slopes it will empty itself once the circulating pump has been switched off. The shelves onto which rocks will be mortared should be about 150 mm (6 in) down from the top edge and at least that width, preferably wider.

Once the concrete has been cast, it should be thoroughly rendered *before* rocks are introduced so that the whole structure is perfectly watertight. If it is easier to run a pipe from the bottom pool up to the top in a direct route than to run it all the way around the outside of the area, it could be installed before concreting so that part of it actually runs beneath the system. Once the whole structure has been rendered, a selection of rocks can be mortared into position wherever a fall or cascade is wanted. These will dam up water behind them so great care must be taken to make sure that when a pool (or stream) is full, the water will flow over these waterfall rocks just before it floods over the sides of the pool.

Rocks chosen for these falls should either already have been partly worn away by water or be 'throated' in some way so that water will flow cleanly over, and not dribble back. The back of these rocks must also be rendered so that water cannot seep down into the next pool when the pump is switched off. There is no danger, however, of water escaping from the overall system since it has all been cast as one. Deep waterfalls could be partly built up with concrete blocks but these should only be used below water level where they cannot be seen. Painting them with a black water resistant paint can often make them look less obtrusive. The bottom pool may need an overflow, more particularly if it is in a part of the garden where indiscriminate flooding would be a nuisance.

As soon as the waterfalls have been completed (but *before* any other rocks are added) the whole system must be filled with water and a pump connected to the delivery pipe and an electricity supply. With the pump running at full volume, a careful check should be made to see that water is flowing properly over the falls and not flooding over any pool or stream edges first. Once all the other rocks have been

Quite large areas of water are needed for traditional water lilies and shelves are useful around the edges for marginal planting.

added it will become very difficult to spot this. Where pool edges are too low, they can easily be built up with a little extra rendering. Once the whole system has been running satisfactorily for a number of hours without loss of water, the remaining rocks can be mortared onto the shelves and other rocks arranged just outside the pools to complete the layout. If soil is brought up behind the pool rocks, care must be taken to prevent soil from connecting with any water which may be flowing in small spaces behind these rocks. Any connection with soil from the surrounding garden will suck water out of the system. These small voids should be backfilled with a non-porous material – perhaps polythene or more mortar/rendering. Where possible, rocks should be arranged with their strata all going the same way (see page 79).

Some of the cascades may be enhanced by the strategic positioning of loose rocks but care is needed to see that water does not then splash uncontrollably out of the system. A project like this re-circulates the same water over and over again, so any loss will result in the levels dropping, especially in the bottom pool, while the pump is running.

Planting

Plants are an important factor and many aquatic and marginal plants can be grown in 'baskets' of soil placed in the water. Some could help to disguise the pump. Outside the pools there will be plenty of opportunities for planting with weeping and prostrate plants being especially useful near the water's edge. Plants will also help to hide the electricity supply and any filter tank.

Fish should not be introduced until the free calcium has been either washed out or sealed harmlessly in.

Pond Within a Pond – *(Fig. 28)*

Construction

This feature needs to be at least 1.5 m (5 ft) across but probably not more than 2.4 m (8 ft). It will not be very deep and water loss through evaporation could be quite noticeable under certain weather conditions. Construction must therefore be thorough so that no water can be lost in any other way. The outer pool is built and made completely watertight before the centre section and upper pool are constructed within it. Bricks must be non-porous stock bricks. They can be made more water repellant by painting them with a clear resin. This applies mainly to those over which water cascades. Any mortar should also be waterproofed with an additive.

'FOAM' FOUNTAIN   The main feature of a 'foam' fountain is achieved by very simply passing a jet of water through a thin layer of water.

Fig. 28 This project, featuring bricks and cobbles, will fit equally well into a modern or traditional setting.

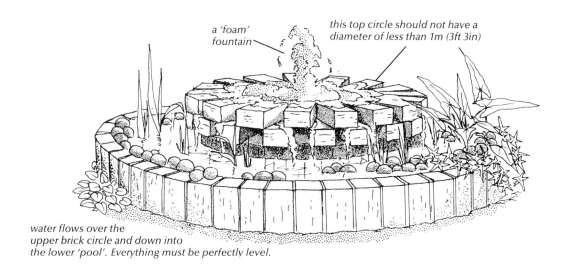

a 'foam' fountain

this top circle should not have a diameter of less than 1m (3ft 3in)

water flows over the upper brick circle and down into the lower 'pool'. Everything must be perfectly level.

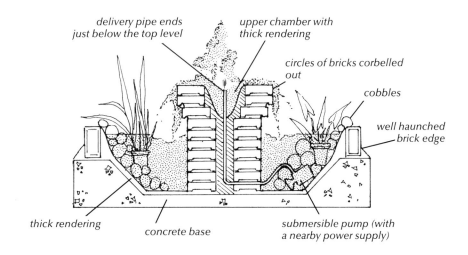

delivery pipe ends just below the top level

upper chamber with thick rendering

circles of bricks corbelled out

cobbles

well haunched brick edge

thick rendering

concrete base

submersible pump (with a nearby power supply)

The upper, inner pool, where this takes place need not be very deep – 250 mm (9 in) would be sufficient. A rigid vertical pipe from the submersible pump situated in the lower (outer) pool is brought up through the centre of this upper pool to within about 5 mm (³⁄₁₆ in) of the rim. This distance below the rim is critical and may need adjusting. If the distance is insufficient, the jet of water will not be checked and will emerge as a strong but uninteresting column of water. Somewhere between will produce an attractive foam effect. Adjustments can be made by sawing small amounts off the end of the vertical pipe as a process of trial and error but this is risky, permanent and irreversible. An adjustable top section to this pipe would offer greater flexibility.

When the pump is switched off, some water in the upper pool will flow back down the pipe, thus lowering the level of the water. The level could drop even further if the pump is left off for several days. When it is switched on again, there will be no water above the pipe and a simple jet of water will shoot up in the air. After a minute or so, the top pool will fill right up and as it does so, a foam-type fountain will develop again.

The submersible pump will have to be concealed in the outer pool with the help of cobble stones and plants. It may, however, become fouled with snails and debris from time to time, especially if it is in relatively shallow water, so it would be sensible to place it where it can be easily reached. Irises and small marginal plants can be planted directly into pockets of soil trapped between cobble stones, or in pots wedged between cobbles. No plants should be placed in the top pool nor right up against the central column. Too much planting will obscure the water.

Note. Special fountain jets are available which actually mix air and water to produce a foam fountain. Although these produce a better and more reliable fountain than the technique described here, they are considerably more expensive. They could, however, be used in this project.

Continuously Flowing Hand Pump – *(Fig. 29)*

This project uses an old-fashioned hand pump which would normally be used to raise water from a well. In recent years, the manufacture of these or similar pumps has been resumed, mainly for use as ornaments or for pumping water out of water butts and similar garden containers. Most are quite large, but small versions are available. A large one is needed here along with a submersible pump and an electricity supply. These hand pumps comprise of at least two separate sections – the main ornamental (working) top section, and a lower section of pipe which would normally go down into a well. Each section ends/begins with a steel flange that has holes which enable the two to be bolted together. The height of the main pump will, therefore, partly depend on the length and type of this lower section.

Plumbing

In this project, the lower section does not itself carry water, only a relatively thin pipe of water on its way up from a submersible pump. At the point where the two sections bolt together, a watertight diaphragm is needed into which the end of the pipe (from the submersible pump) can be plumbed. The idea is to fill the top section from this point, so that when full, it simply overflows out of the spout. This produces a much more realistic effect than simply running the delivery pipe right up through the top section and straight into the spout.

A diaphragm can be made from a range of materials but probably the best will be one which allows the end of the delivery pipe to be plumbed in using normal plumbing collars and washers. A slightly flexible plastic similar to that used in the manufacture of domestic water tanks will work well, but grease or mastic sealant is needed between the circle of plastic and the steel flanges. Once the end of the delivery pipe has been plumbed into the circle of plastic and the two flanges bolted together, there should be no need to open it up again except, perhaps, for very occasional cleaning.

Fixing the pump

The height at which the main pump is mounted depends partly on what the water is to flow into. This could be, for example, a large barrel, a mock well, or a small pool. This 'reservoir' may be the main – probably the only – source of water, so it should not be too small. It will also have to accommodate the submersible pump. A two-stage reservoir could be used with the water from the hand pump flowing initially into something like an old-fashioned watering can or bucket, then, by way of a concealed overflow, continue on into a large concealed underground reservoir (see page 75). If the intermediate stage is something like a watering can, there is a danger that, on windy days, the water from the hand pump could miss its target and spill. This will not matter too much if the watering can is standing on some form of grill over the reservoir below; any spillage will then simply go straight down into this reservoir and be re-cycled.

All pipework must be thoroughly hidden, including perhaps the bottom section of the pump which can look unsightly.

When this bottom section of pipe is used to draw water from a well, it is often concreted into position and can, therefore, be relied upon to provide significant support to the main part of the pump. In these ornamental projects, this might not be the case, so a stout post or wall mounting would have to be arranged.

Once fitted together, this project should require little maintenance.

If problems do occur, they will probably be with water blowing out of the system on windy days or perhaps from a faulty joint where the two flanges have been bolted together.

In the case of a two-tier reservoir, arrangements will have to be made that enable you to see if the water level is running low and make it easy to remove the pump for servicing. Depending upon the circumstances, planting can be a very important part of the overall effect, especially if the intention is to create a 'cottage garden' corner with tubs, hanging baskets and cottage garden flowers or herbs.

Fig. 29 This traditional hand pump can easily be fixed to pour water continuously into a tub or similar receptacle.

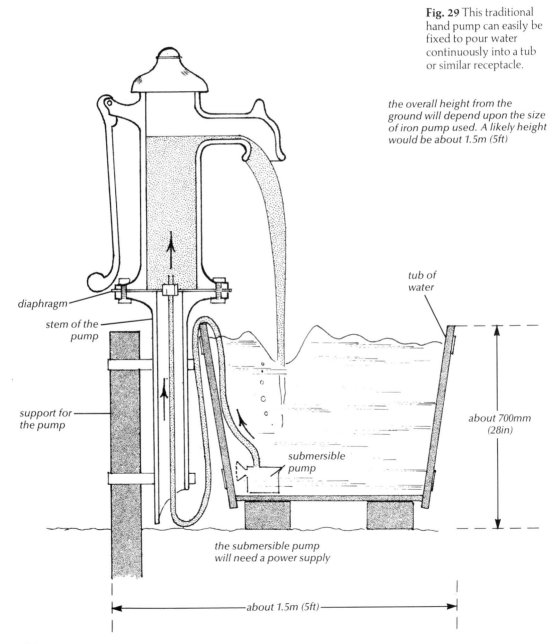

the overall height from the ground will depend upon the size of iron pump used. A likely height would be about 1.5m (5ft)

diaphragm

stem of the pump

support for the pump

tub of water

submersible pump

about 700mm (28in)

the submersible pump will need a power supply

about 1.5m (5ft)

Water Flowing from a Wall – *(Fig. 30)*

Like most of the other water projects, this is an illusion. Only part of the pool, into which water flows, is visible. The rest exists behind a wall. The whole scheme will have to tie in with an existing or intended garden retaining wall. It would look unconvincing if only a short, isolated piece of wall 'backed' the pool. It is obviously easiest to start from scratch and build a new wall at the same time as the pool but it would also be possible to demolish a section of existing wall so that a pool could be built, then rebuild afterwards.

Fig. 30(a) Water flows continously from a wall, re-cycled from the pond below.

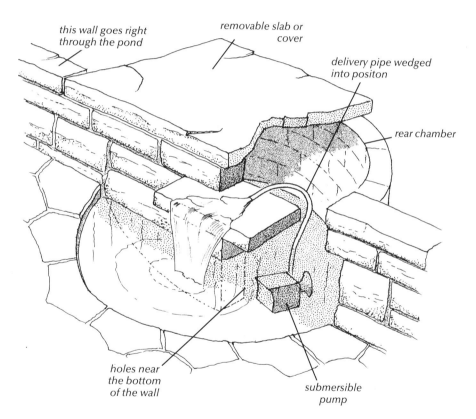

this wall goes right through the pond

removable slab or cover

delivery pipe wedged into positon

rear chamber

holes near the bottom of the wall

submersible pump

Pool

This can have vertical sides built from concrete blocks on top of a concrete raft base, or it could be built from free-form concrete (together with steel reinforcing) with slightly sloping sides. Both must be perfectly level. Once the pool has been built a wall will, in effect, go right through the centre of it, so before this can happen the pool must be made completely watertight. In actual fact, only a small section of water is needed behind the wall so, depending on the overall size of the project, the wall is more likely to divide the pool roughly into one third and two thirds, not in half.

Wall

This can be built from brick or stone – stone usually being the most successful. Water has to flow freely from one side to the other so gaps must be left through the bottom of the wall (well below the water line). At some point above the water, probably quite close to the top of the wall, a slit is needed with a sill, over which water can flow cleanly down into the pool below. This sill should be quite deep so that about 75 mm (3 in) can protrude from the front of the wall and about 225 mm (9 in) reach back inside. Apart from passing through the 'centre' of the pool, the wall will also have to be built up around the back, on top of the pool, so that there is something on which a lid can rest. This portion of wall does not, however, have to be made watertight since it will all be above water level.

One of the more difficult aspects of this project is to find pieces of stone large enough to make a lid right over the back part of the pool yet still appear as part of the wall. Since a submersible pump will be housed in this back portion, the lid should leave a small space for the electric cable and be removable so that the pump can be serviced.

Waterflow

A short length of flexible pipe is attached to the pump outflow and brought up to the back of the sill where it can be wedged into position with a suitable piece of stone. With the pump running, the position of the pipe can be adjusted until the flow of water is right. The further back the sill reaches, the more scope there is for adjustment before the water finally reaches and flows over the front edge. The pump obviously draws water from the main front part of the pond through gaps left in the wall. Unfortunately fish may spend more time behind the wall than in front but this can often be solved by fitting some form of filter material in the gaps.

The stone used in the wall must not be too porous, otherwise it will gradually suck water out into the surrounding garden. Its porosity can be significantly reduced by spraying several coats of colourless silicone front and back. The pool itself is likely to have a paved surround, and because the wall is likely to be a retaining wall, much of the planting will be above it. Prostrate and spreading plants are the most useful in helping to hide the lid which, in some cases, may be quite extensive. These plants will also cascade over the walls and help to integrate this feature with the surrounding garden.

Overflow

This particular water feature would look rather silly if water flooded over the paved surround after heavy rain, so an overflow which will prevent this yet enable the level to rise to the lower edge of the paving is needed.

This pool, with its sound of water flowing from the wall, is ideal for the edge of a patio. Its construction can be seen in Fig. 30.

Fig. 30b shows, on the left, a conventional overflow which will work but which does not allow the pond to fill to the top. The arrangement on the right overcomes this problem and allows the pond to fill right up before overflowing.

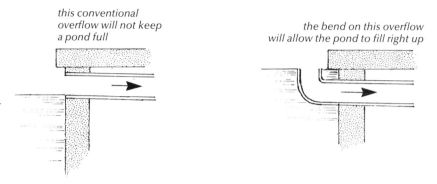

this conventional overflow will not keep a pond full

the bend on this overflow will allow the pond to fill right up

Fig. 30(b) A pond overflow can be arranged to allow the pond to fill right to the top before overflowing.

Millstone Bubble Fountain – *(Fig. 31)*

Although this feature is widely used in all sorts of situations, it is not in itself very original. The technology which it uses can, however, be applied to a much wider range of ideas. Of all the features shown so far it is possibly the safest for very young children because there is no significant depth of water within reach.

Millstone

Sometimes real millstones are used but these are not always easy to find. An alternative, which is often easier to buy is a thick, millstone-shaped piece of rock which has had a hole drilled through the centre and its top carved out into a shallow dish. It is possible to buy hollow, manufactured versions of these stones and although they are much lighter, they are often considerably more expensive.

Apart from the millstone, cobble stones, a submersible pump, an electricity supply and a reservoir are needed.

Reservoir

This should be significantly larger than the millstone. As a rough guide, the reservoir ought to be at least 300 mm (12 in) wider than the millstone all round so that water cascading down over the edges cannot easily splash outside the system. It should also be strong enough to withstand considerable weight both from the millstone and the cobble stones.

The ideal reservoir is a large, circular plastic or fibreglass tank at least 400 mm (16 in) deep, but it is not always possible to locate one which is large enough. A tank made from concrete blocks set on a circular concrete foundation and rendered is another possibility but obviously involves quite a lot of work and expense. Both tanks would have vertical or almost vertical sides. An alternative is to line a moderately steep-sided excavation with butyl sheeting but precautions will have to be taken to avoid damage. Among these are a layer of soft sand under the liner and extra layers of butyl or some other protective material, wherever heavy weights or sharp edges come into contact with it. A combination is also possible: a concrete block structure lined with butyl and a felt underlay. In all cases, the top edge of the reservoir should be just below normal ground level.

Supporting the millstone

Both the millstone and the cobbles will have to be suspended level with the top of the reservoir. This could be done with steel bars or a steel grid spanning across the top, but the gaps are likely to be too wide to support the cobble stones. The pump will have to be serviced from time to time and the gaps between the bars or the grid may be too small for this. Columns of bricks could support the millstone but not the cobbles and will take up quite a lot of space which could otherwise be occupied by water. One solution is to fill the reservoir (as far as is possible) with upturned polypropylene crates or baskets which are strong yet leave plenty of room for water. A space can easily be left for a pump, and a steel mesh or grille laid across the top to support the cobbles and the millstone. A small section of this grille will have to be removable so that the pump can be serviced. The steel will also have to be thoroughly painted with red oxide and perhaps a waterproof paint on top of this. At every stage the reservoir must be protected from sharp edges and the effect of heavy weights. Another

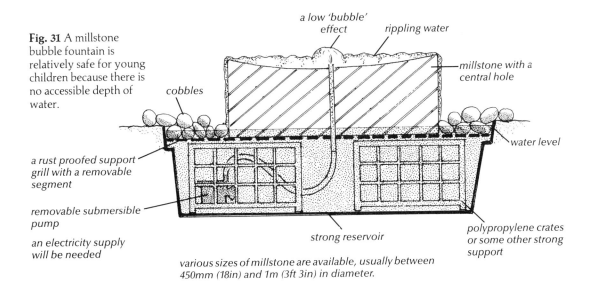

Fig. 31 A millstone bubble fountain is relatively safe for young children because there is no accessible depth of water.

a low 'bubble' effect

rippling water

millstone with a central hole

cobbles

a rust proofed support grill with a removable segment

removable submersible pump

an electricity supply will be needed

water level

strong reservoir

polypropylene crates or some other strong support

various sizes of millstone are available, usually between 450mm (18in) and 1m (3ft 3in) in diameter.

advantage of these crates or baskets is that they will support a large proportion of the feature so that if someone stands on the cobbles, the grille should not give way.

Dipstick

This is a useful addition. A narrow rigid tube can be fixed down into the bottom of the reservoir and protrude discreetly between cobble stones. A stick is then lowered into the tube to see how much water is left – submersible pumps can be damaged if there is not enough water around them.

Bubble fountain

It is important to use a pump which can be controlled and kept down to quite a low ouput. Water will emerge from a piece of rigid piping set just above the surface of the stone but a little below the rim of the dish so that when the feature is running, the top of the pipe is just below water level. The pump must be set so that only a low jet of water emerges from the pipe – not more than 75 mm (3 in) high. This is not enough to produce a 'foam' fountain but should be sufficient to give a bubbly effect, together with concentric ripples which will be constantly moving outwards from the centre. Water obviously flows over and down the sides of the millstone into the reservoir below. If

the millstone has been hollowed out into quite a deep dish it may be possible to run the pump faster and produce a 'foam'-type fountain (see page 66). With such gentle movement of water, fallen leaves and other debris can quickly spoil the effect so it is not a particularly suitable feature for beneath trees. The top of the millstone must be kept clean and be set precisely level for the best results. The rigid pipe which passes through the millstone will need a bend near the base so that a good length of flexible piping can be fixed to it and the pump. When the pump needs servicing, the small removable section of grill can be opened (after removing some cobble stones) and the pump taken out on its long length of flexible piping. It can then be detached from this and taken away. An electric cable will also, of course, go down into the reservoir from a nearby post and all-weather socket.

Planting

The area of cobble stones is often extended beyond the water feature into the soil around. This provides an excellent opportunity to plant many ornamental grasses, dwarf bamboos, yuccas and phormiums, all of which associate well with water and this type of feature. Very tall plants should, however, be used with care since they have the potential to hide everything.

Lighting, if placed nearby, can produce some very attractive night-time effects, particularly if it can be aimed at the moving water.

Millstone water features always look effective in association with beach stones and fit well into quite small areas. See Fig. 31 for construction.

Chapter 6

Rock Gardens

Rock Garden on a Natural Bank – *(Fig. 32)*

There are obviously many different types of rock, and their basic character will dictate what type of rock feature is possible. The rock used here is mainly large block-shaped pieces which can produce taller

Fig. 32 This rock garden incorporates a grotto, scree bed, steps, path and a sunken area, along with plenty of planting spaces.

pool and grotto

a sunken area

and more angular features than rock which is available only in very flat, craggy pieces. It is always, therefore, important to have some idea of what the finished project is to look like before finally deciding on the type of rock to use.

Strata

Nearly all rock has lines of weakness or 'strata' running through it and here some attempt has been made to ensure that these lines are arranged in the same direction throughout the feature.

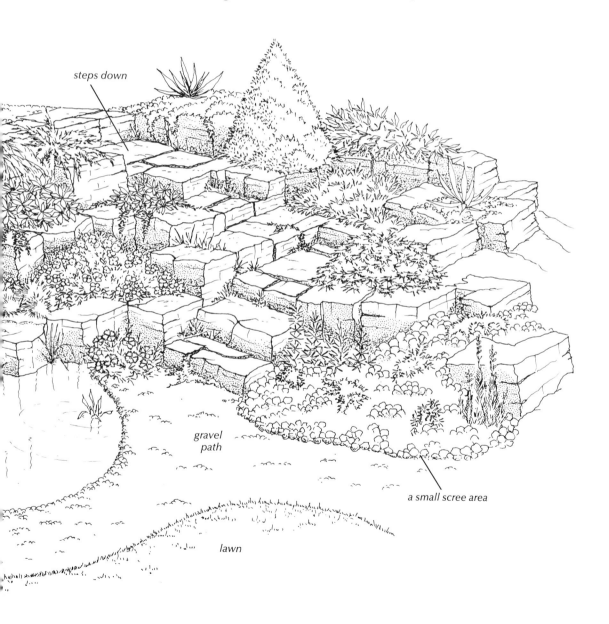

steps down

gravel path

a small scree area

lawn

Outcrop – *(Fig. 33a and b)*

This is a cluster of rocks grouped in such a way as to look as if one huge boulder, buried beneath the ground, has been partly exposed. In this feature it was decided to give the impression that several outcrops of this boulder have been exposed. It is obviously very important to make sure that these are all arranged at a similar angle or tilt and that the strata is all running the same way.

Fig. 33(a) Building height with rocks.

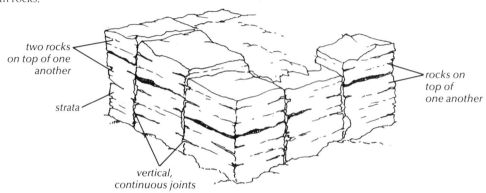

two rocks on top of one another

strata

vertical, continuous joints

rocks on top of one another

(b) Rock outcrops and terraces on a natural bank.

Construction would have begun at the bottom of the existing slope, the first rocks to be used being fairly large and set at an appropriate tilt or angle with a slight backward lean. There is a temptation to line up all the rocks so that they produce almost straight terraces, which can look boring and un-natural. If the first rocks (key stones) are set at an angle to the line of vision, this will force construction to progress backwards in two different directions, producing sharply angled outcrops with pronounced 'ins' and 'outs'. This has given the feature an interesting three-dimensional effect. As work progressed back into the bank, it would have been possible to build some of the outcrops quite high while others were kept low. To create any appreciable height, rocks have to be built on top of one another. This must be done with vertical joints running from top to bottom as if the huge 'boulder' has developed deep cracks. They should not be staggered or bonded like bricks in a wall.

It is difficult to plan the exact course of a rock feature but sometimes it can help to make a small model in a box or tray using soil and pieces of bark (or angular stones) to represent rocks. The general position of valleys, ravines, grottoes, high spots and so on, can be quite easily shown, giving you something to work towards.

Any type of rock can be used but very soft sandstones may break up rather easily in frost or erode away in wetter districts.

Planting pockets

One major purpose of a rock garden feature is to provide a home for alpine plants. Some of these need well drained areas, others damp crevices. Some prefer shade and others like full sun. Here all sorts of crevices and pockets, together with some scree, have been included so that a wide selection of plants could be grown.

Scree

This is an area of broken rocks or stone with little or no soil. Under natural conditions, huge areas of scree can build up at the foot of mountains as a result of erosion. Pieces break off and cascade down to form huge sweeps of 'scree'. Certain types of alpine plants thrive under these almost soilless, moistureless conditions, so beds of scree could be created around a rock feature to accommodate them. The most convincing-looking scree beds are built at the foot of the larger outcrops with the largest pieces of broken rock at the bottom and the smallest near the top and around the outside to mimic the pattern formed by naturally accumulated scree. A scree does not necessarily have to be very deep – 150 mm (6 in) or so is usually enough to provide the special conditions needed.

Scree plants often need protecting from heavy rain during the winter. This can be achieved by erecting a single sheet of glass as a sloping roof above them.

Steps

Here large, block-shaped pieces of rock have been used for steps, with extra stone packed in behind to complete each tread. Their size obviously varies and they have been arranged to go around corners adding charm and interest. Carpeting-type alpines would be planted in the corners and adjacent crevices to grow out gradually across the treads and spill over the edges.

Grotto

The grotto (cave) is not necessarily large enough to crawl inside. Water might often drip from the roof into the shallow pebble pool below, which may extend a little way outside the grotto. The roof could be supported by steel or reinforced concrete beams, but if steel is used, it must be thoroughly painted with a rust proofer. Sometimes it is possible to find rocks large enough to span the roof, more particularly across the entrance, but it is vital that the roof is reliably strong and that any artificial materials are well disguised.

This grotto has been created in an especially steep part of the rock garden but could have been built into a bank as a completely separate feature somewhere else in a garden. If necessary, the back and sides can be first built up with concrete blocks (mortared) to prevent soil from moving forward. Smaller pieces of stone can then be mortared in front while the concrete blocks provide the main structural strength.

There are areas of planting all around the grotto, and especially plants growing down from the top which will help to integrate it with the surrounding garden.

Sunken rock feature

Where soil drainage is good, above-ground outcrops can be extended down below ground. One of these has been incorporated on the left-hand end of this rock garden rather like a mock, dry river bed. The main structural rocks should still follow any angles and strata visible in surrounding outcrops but other, smaller rocks, could be tipped in here and there to give a semi-scree effect. At one point a bridge might cross an area like this. Even in well drained soils, the ditch is likely to retain more moisture than other, more elevated areas of rocks and will, therefore, extend the range of plants which can be grown.

The construction of this feature would have begun at the front and foot of the natural slope, with the sunken area being excavated early on so that the soil could be used elsewhere. The grotto, pool and steps will have caused a lot of disruption with the movement of heavy materials back and forth so these too would have been early jobs. The gravel path would be one of the last structural jobs, followed by the topsoiling and planting of the various beds, pockets and crevices.

Grottoes like this can be particularly effective with coloured night lighting and trickling water. This one is in a small sloping garden.

82

Tufa

In a smaller rock garden tufa could be used in selected areas. This is a highly porous, soft and lightweight rock which is full of tiny holes. Many alpine plants, including those which grow in scree, will thrive if planted into holes drilled out of the tufa. No soil is necessary, just ground-up tufa.

Rock features on a flat site – *(Fig. 34)*

Here this has been dealt with by building rock outcrops, steps and so on, on the 'front' side (creating whatever slopes are necessary) and giving it an almost vertical dry stone wall behind. As this wall gradually extends around the sides, it would be reduced in height and integrated with the various rocky features. The overall effect can be further enhanced by having some fairly tall, mainly evergreen shrubby planting behind so that the isolated nature of the whole feature is a little less obvious.

Fig. 34 Creating a rock feature in a flat garden.

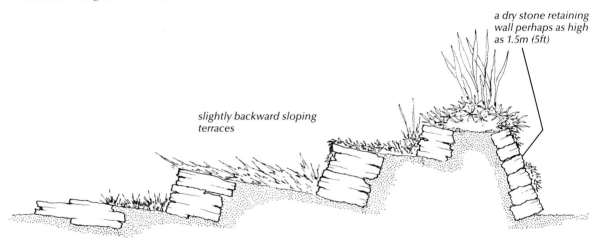

a dry stone retaining wall perhaps as high as 1.5m (5ft)

slightly backward sloping terraces

Moving heavy rocks

This can be difficult and dangerous. Gloves and hard-toe boots help but there are one or two techniques which can make the job easier. Rocks can be carried on a wide plank moving across rollers made from lengths of pole at least 75 mm (3 in) thick. As long as the rollers are really thick, it will be very easy to move very heavy rocks across quite a soft lawn without any appreciable damage. A strong two-wheeled porter's trolley wheeled along planks also works very well but a single-wheeled barrow can be particularly dangerous if it goes off balance with a heavy rock. Large projects may benefit from the use of a crane. This might sound rather 'over the top' but the saving on hard work, and damage to the garden, may make it a really worthwhile investment.

Chapter 7

Timber in the Garden

Although each project in this chapter is described in detail, some general points are common to them all.

Types of Timber

These fall into two main categories: hardwoods and softwoods.

Hardwoods

In general, these are close and fine grained (least likely to splinter), often able to resist decay with their natural resins or oils and, as the name implies, are quite hard. They are not all easy to work with since some have a tendency to split or chip. Most have a pleasing colour and need only surface treatment with waxes, oils or synthetic products which are used merely to enhance the natural colour and resilience. Hardwoods are ideal for use in timber decking, handrails and garden furniture – all situations where splintering would be particularly undesirable. Very often, hardwoods are relatively expensive.

   Included among hardwoods is oak, teak, eroko, mahogany, beech etc. Redwood, cedar and thuya are often classed as hardwoods because of their notable resistance to decay, but from a working point of view, cedar in particular can be very soft and easily damaged.

Softwoods

These tend to splinter more than hardwoods and have a more open grain. Although softer than many hardwoods, most softwoods are strong and highly suitable for many types of construction. In their natural state, softwoods tend to decay quickly in the soil and need treatment if they are to last a realistic length of time in the garden. The problem of decay has been largely overcome in recent years by the use of highly effective and persistent preservatives. The most thorough method of applying these substances is pressure treatment where the timber is put into a pressure chamber with the chemical. This does, however, saturate it and certain chemicals may produce a slight discolouration – bluish green is the most common. If the wet timber is not being used for a while, it should be strapped firmly together in bundles with some spacing blocks to allow air movement. Drying out should be allowed to take place only gradually. Pressure treatment will probably keep the timber free from decay for twenty years or so. An alternative to pressure treatment is spraying the timber with a penetrating preservative.

Colouring timber

Some preservatives are brown and, therefore, colour the timber at the same time as preserving it. If a different colour is wanted, the best approach is to use a colourless, or almost colourless preservative, then follow up with a suitable stain.

Sawn timber

When a log is cut up in a saw mill, the resulting rough-surfaced timber is referred to as 'sawn timber'. Hardwoods, because of their dense structure do in fact come out of this process feeling relatively smooth but softwood will feel rough and full of splinters. It is the sawn soft-wood which is normally pressure treated. Once this has been carried out, it is usually difficult to obtain a really smooth finish with planing.

Prepared or planed timber

This describes timber which has been through the further process of planing to produce a smooth surface. Where timber is being used for furniture or decking, whether it be hardwood or softwood, planing is advisable. Planed timber is not much more expensive than sawn and the dimensions are a little smaller as a result of the planing. Planed timber is not usually pressure treated as standard but more usually as a special order, and again, care will be needed to make sure it does not warp as it dries out.

Wood which has been cut from the centre of a tree is the least likely to warp, is often referred to as heart wood and is usually the most expensive. Wood cut from the outer parts of a tree may warp more readily and could well have more 'knots'. Knots in thin strips of timber can produce a weakness so all timber should be either selected in the timber yard or checked on delivery.

Fixings – *(Fig. 35)*

Fixings for individual situations are discussed under each project. There are, however, some general points which can be applied to most of the projects. Where two pieces of timber are to be fixed together so that they cannot *pull* apart, screws or bolts should be used. In the case of decking or panelling, nails or pins can be used but

Fig. 35 Some useful timber fixings.

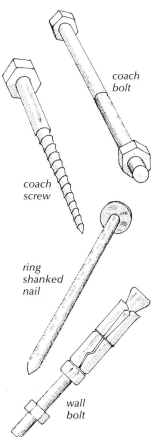

coach bolt

coach screw

ring shanked nail

wall bolt

should be put in at an angle so that they cannot pull out so easily. Where two surfaces must be prevented from shearing apart, bolts are often preferable to screws although 'coach' screws, which are wound in with a spanner, can be very effective for large-scale work. Ordinary screws will suffice only for light loads and small-scale work. Friction is an important factor where two surfaces must be prevented from shearing and often a simple joint or roughened surface in conjunction with bolts or screws can significantly increase strength.

Where one piece of timber resting upon another merely needs stabilizing, nails can be used. Occasionally weatherproof/waterproof adhesives can be used but usually only in small-scale work (for example, in garden furniture) and always in conjunction with screws, bolts or nails. Where timber has to be fixed to walls, a whole range of bolts and screws is available – some using an expanding bolt principle and others being based on the idea of a plastic plug and screw.

Working with Rustic Timber

In some garden settings, rustic structures are more appropriate than structures made from sawn timber. Choosing the most appropriate type of rustic material will depend, to some extent, on the type of project involved. Victorian-style rustic work, for example, was very ornate and relied heavily on the natural bends and twists of oak branches set within a fairly straight-sided framework. Modern rustic work is based on much straighter and more precise lengths of pole, usually of conifer origin.

Modern rustic poles

The advantage of modern poles is that, under some circumstances, they can be pressure treated to last many years, but this can only be carried out on poles which have had their bark removed. Sweet chestnut (*Castanea sativa*) is very resistant to decay and does not really need pressure treating. It can therefore be used with its bark left on. Oak too is very resilient but seldom straight enough to be used as uprights. These could be chestnut.

If it is preferred to use other poles with their bark left on, they could be treated just on the ends which will be going into the ground. The bark will have to be stripped from enough of the pole to ensure treatment can reach just above ground level. Stripped ends of poles are stood for at least 48 hours in a deep reservoir of penetrating preservative (not creosote).

Alternatively, these ends should be charred in a fire. Either treatment will provide some protection from bacteria in the soil. Those untreated, bark-covered poles in the air will have to take their chance although, once again, chestnut is likely to last longest.

Rustic poles are often used in the construction of a wide range of garden structures, although joints have to be relatively simple and may not, therefore, be particularly strong. Long straight lengths of tall trellis can be vulnerable to wind damage because joints will have a degree of flexibility. Here the uprights should be put deep into the ground for stability, but structures like arches and pergolas can be given cross braces around the top for extra strength.

Joints

Wherever two rounded surfaces are brought together, a slight flattening of each will produce a much better union. The same applies where the end of one pole comes up against the side of another. Although thick structural poles might be fixed together with long bolts, most fixing is done with nails. Galvanized nails provide a more secure union than bright steel – ring-shanked nails are even better but often restricted in the length available.

Timber sizes

Sizes usually relate to the diameter (thickness) across the top of the poles. Uprights, for example, would often have a top diameter of 75–100 mm (3–4 in), and cross beams a diameter of 50–75 mm (2–3 in). Thinner pieces can be used but become increasingly difficult to nail. Oak, in particular, may split if too large a nail is used.

Cutting

The best saw is a coarse-toothed panel saw or, if the timber is very wet, a small bow saw with a tight blade. A chisel will be needed to create some flat surfaces.

The rustic projects shown in Fig. 36 are a mixture of old and new.

'Old' rustic arch – *(Fig. 36a)*

The 'Victorian' arch could comprise of just two poles and a single bowed branch across the top, or be more three-dimensional with four

Fig. 36 Examples of Victorian rustic work using mainly oak and apple with perhaps sweet chestnut uprights. **(a)** Gateway and fencing.

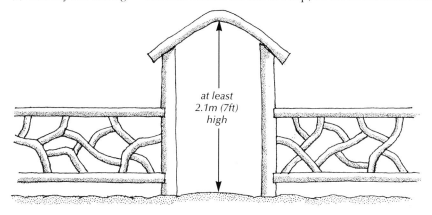

at least
2.1m (7ft)

(b) Modern rustic work using smooth, straight poles.

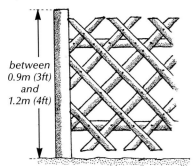

between
0.9m (3ft)
and
1.2m (4ft)

cross poles
simply laid
on and nailed

(c) Balustrade.

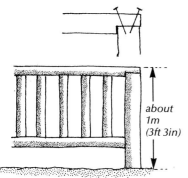

about
1m
(3ft 3in)

(d)A Victorian planter, designed in about 1880.

posts and a matrix of branches across the top. A degree of cunning is necessary to ensure that it is always possible to bang in the nails for the trellis work! Oak or apple would have been the most likely types of wood for this sort of project years ago. Today the uprights could be sweet chestnut or tanalized softwood for extra durability.

The modern criss-cross screen and balustrading are both easy to construct.

Criss-cross screen – *(Fig. 36b)*

This has a basic framework of uprights and horizontal poles, to which the diagonals are attached. These would be nailed right through into the horizontal bars but because they are relatively thin (35–50 mm or 1½–2 in) they should be pre-drilled to prevent splitting. Galvanized or ring-shanked nails are best.

Balustrade – *(Fig. 36c)*

Again, this is based on a framework of uprights (going into the ground) and two horizontal bars which must be fixed firmly together for maximum strength. The structure will be that much stronger if the ends of these bars can be inset slightly into the horizontal ones.

'Victorian' planter – *(Fig 36d)*

Here is a copy of one designed around 1880. The method of construction is not quite how the Victorians would have built it, but the end result will be very similar. It could be made any height between 1.2 m and 1.5 m (4–5 ft) and accommodate ivy and some bedding plants.

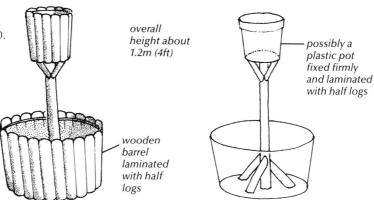

overall
height about
1.2m (4ft)

possibly a
plastic pot
fixed firmly
and laminated
with half logs

wooden
barrel
laminated
with half
logs

Modern sawn trellis

The trellis work shown in Fig. 37 uses treated, planed timber measuring 33 mm × 22 mm (1¼ in × 1 in). In order to achieve a flush finish, nearly all the joints will have to be 'half lap'. These are held

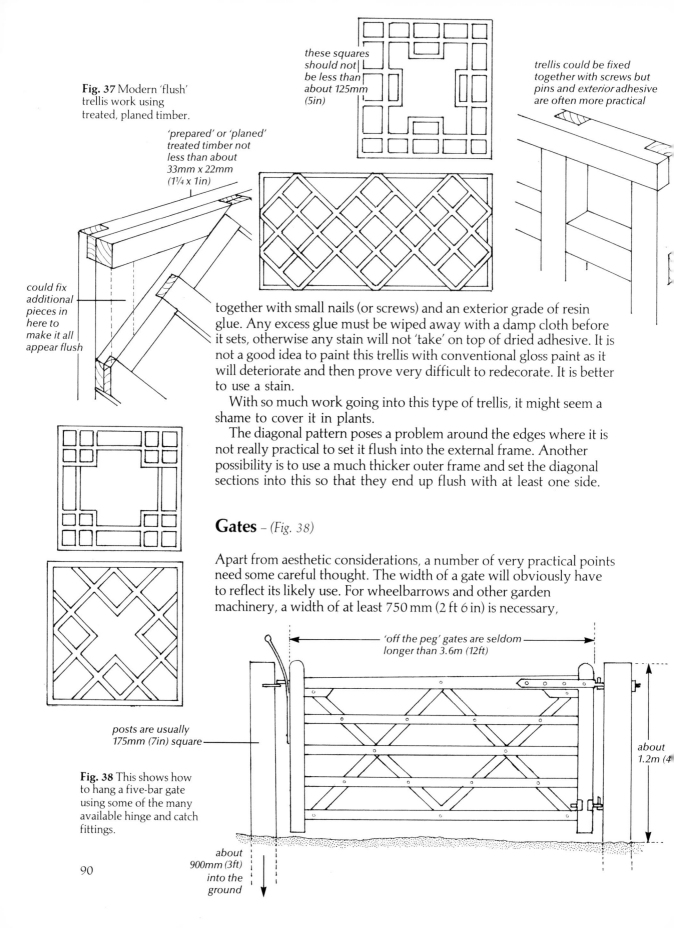

Fig. 37 Modern 'flush' trellis work using treated, planed timber.

these squares should not be less than about 125mm (5in)

trellis could be fixed together with screws but pins and *exterior* adhesive are often more practical

'prepared' or 'planed' treated timber not less than about 33mm x 22mm (1¼ x 1in)

could fix additional pieces in here to make it all appear flush

together with small nails (or screws) and an exterior grade of resin glue. Any excess glue must be wiped away with a damp cloth before it sets, otherwise any stain will not 'take' on top of dried adhesive. It is not a good idea to paint this trellis with conventional gloss paint as it will deteriorate and then prove very difficult to redecorate. It is better to use a stain.

With so much work going into this type of trellis, it might seem a shame to cover it in plants.

The diagonal pattern poses a problem around the edges where it is not really practical to set it flush into the external frame. Another possibility is to use a much thicker outer frame and set the diagonal sections into this so that they end up flush with at least one side.

Gates – *(Fig. 38)*

Apart from aesthetic considerations, a number of very practical points need some careful thought. The width of a gate will obviously have to reflect its likely use. For wheelbarrows and other garden machinery, a width of at least 750 mm (2 ft 6 in) is necessary,

'off the peg' gates are seldom longer than 3.6m (12ft)

posts are usually 175mm (7in) square

about 1.2m (4

Fig. 38 This shows how to hang a five-bar gate using some of the many available hinge and catch fittings.

about 900mm (3ft) into the ground

90

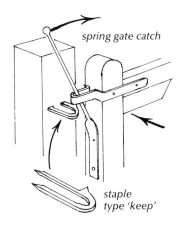

spring gate catch

staple
type 'keep'

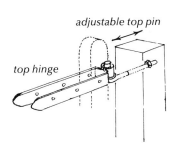

adjustable top pin

top hinge

adjustable
bottom hinge

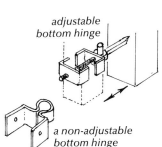

a non-adjustable
bottom hinge

preferably more. The way a gate opens (its handedness) is also important. A long five-bar gate, for example, could jam on the ground if it opens back onto a hillside. It may not be practical to have it opening the other way, so a pair of smaller gates might work better. An alternative would be to set the large gate higher off the ground but obviously, in its closed position, it would not offer very good security along the bottom. Solid gates do help to reduce draughts blowing down narrow passageways but they can also shut out a lot of light. One practical solution is to use a wrought-iron gate and fix a sheet of acrylic onto it so that it is draught proof but will let the light through.

Fences and Screens

In some districts there are by-laws and covenants controlling the erection and height of fences, so this point will need checking with the authorities. It is important to identify what the fence or screen is to achieve:

(*i*) act as a token barrier to intruders and therefore be only knee high?
(*ii*) be a complete barrier to intruders and solid, to prevent any viewing?
(*iii*) be a complete barrier but partially 'see-through'?
(*iv*) act as a partial or complete windbreak?
(*v*) provide privacy just to limited areas of the garden?
(*vi*) divide a garden into smaller sections or 'rooms'?
(*vii*) provide somewhere for climbing plants to grow?
(*viii*) keep out cattle, deer etc?
(*ix*) keep in animals and children?
(*x*) merely to give a token indication of a boundary line?

Once the type of fence or screen has been decided, a pleasing design can, if necessary, be built in. It is important to identify the exact position of a boundary (especially in small gardens) and to make sure that no part of the fence, not even the uprights, go over the line. With closeboard fencing, it is customary to have the triangular arris rails on the owner's side but this is not necessarily a legal requirement.

In windy districts fences and screens must be made especially sturdy, with trellis in particular being given more frequent supports. Plants growing on trellis significantly increase wind resistance and the risk of damage.

Where a new fence is to replace an old one and the old rotten uprights have been set in concrete, it is possible to proceed without removing the old concrete. The new fence can begin with a half panel so that new posts will fall between the old ones. Another half panel may, of course, be required at the end of the run too.

Arches, Pergolas and Gazebos

Although it is relatively easy to define what an arch is, deciding when an arch becomes a pergola and when a pergola becomes a gazebo is not so clear cut. The projects described and illustrated here are probably best described as pergolas although, with some minor modifications, the octagonal pergola could easily become a gazebo.

Gazebo

This is often a rounded structure, sometimes raised above ground level, which has been positioned to take advantage of a certain view across a garden or surrounding countryside. The lower half may well be partly enclosed by a wall or trellis and the top half is usually built to take climbing plants. The floor is either paving or timber decking with space for some garden furniture.

Pergola

This is either a walkway joining two parts of a garden or an arrangement of timber beams spanning an area of paving where garden furniture or a barbecue can be set up. Although the ideas described here are built from wood (with some brickwork) other materials, like steel, can also be used to produce similar structures.

Proportion is all important for structures such as pergolas and gazebos, so a scale drawing should always be made first to ascertain what width and height would look right with various widths and thicknesses of timber. If this is not done, the finished structure might turn out too tall and narrow, short, too heavy, or even too feeble in relation to its surroundings.

Octagonal Pergola – *(Fig. 39)*

This can be quite large because it incorporates a central support. The timber uprights and the ends of the main beams have all been shaped to provide extra style. There are no cross braces, so stability will have to come from good, tight joints around the top and firm fixings at the base of each upright. These uprights could be concreted direct into the ground but may decay rather quickly unless they are treated regularly. Alternatively, you can use steel 'shoes' or sockets concreted into the ground. These would have to be quite deep and substantial, with bolt or screw holes. The posts must fit tightly into these sockets with bolts or screws. Any paving beneath the pergola should be kept at least 300 mm (12 in) away from the uprights so that there is also space for vigorous climbers, like roses, to develop without hitching on to passers-by. Likewise, the pergola should be at least 2.1 m (7 ft) high so that climbers are held above head height.

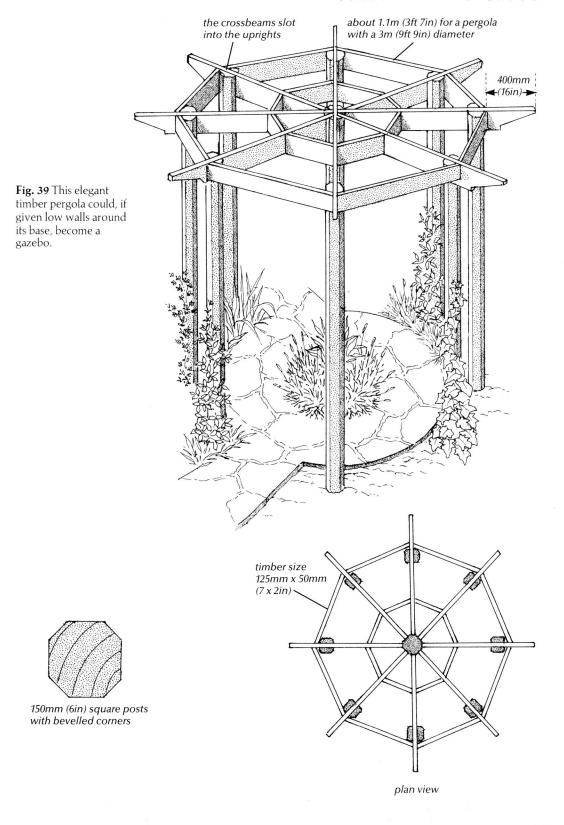

the crossbeams slot into the uprights

about 1.1m (3ft 7in) for a pergola with a 3m (9ft 9in) diameter

400mm (16in)

Fig. 39 This elegant timber pergola could, if given low walls around its base, become a gazebo.

timber size 125mm x 50mm (7 x 2in)

150mm (6in) square posts with bevelled corners

plan view

Pergola Walkway – *(Fig. 40)*

Once again, finding the right proportion is important. This particular structure uses a lot of timber and interlocking joints. Its height must, again, be at least 2.1 m (7 ft). If the width alone is significantly reduced, the structure could appear too tall and narrow and the timber beams may end up so close together as to become oppressive. Reducing timber thicknesses might help.

Uprights must be fixed firmly into the ground because there are no cross braces to give side to side stability. Although nearly all the joints are interlocking, bolts should be incorporated wherever possible to tighten the main joints. The edges of the path must, again, be at least 300 mm (12 in) in from the uprights to give room for plant development.

Fig. 40 A pergola walkway for larger gardens, requiring a good deal of skilful but relatively simple joinery.

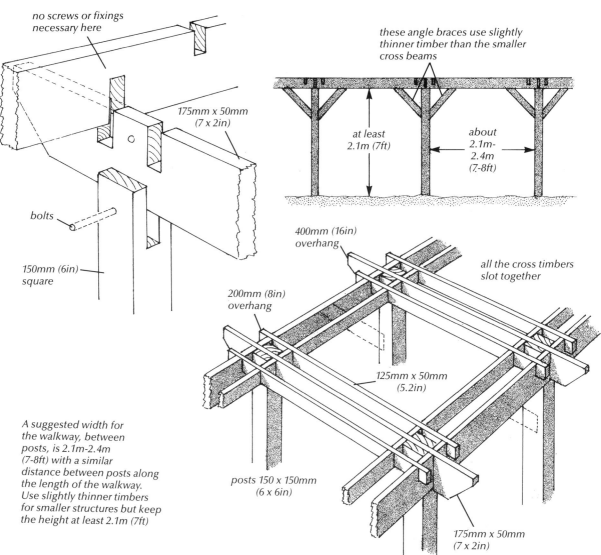

no screws or fixings necessary here

175mm x 50mm (7 x 2in)

bolts

150mm (6in) square

these angle braces use slightly thinner timber than the smaller cross beams

at least 2.1m (7ft)

about 2.1m-2.4m (7-8ft)

400mm (16in) overhang

200mm (8in) overhang

all the cross timbers slot together

125mm x 50mm (5.2in)

posts 150 x 150mm (6 x 6in)

175mm x 50mm (7 x 2in)

A suggested width for the walkway, between posts, is 2.1m-2.4m (7-8ft) with a similar distance between posts along the length of the walkway. Use slightly thinner timbers for smaller structures but keep the height at least 2.1m (7ft)

Above: The timberwork in this octagonal pergola needs to be particularly chunky so that it not only looks solid but can support heavy climbers.

Left: This shows part of the pergola walkway (Fig. 40) and how interlocking joints help to keep the reliance on screws, bolts and nails to a minimum.

Cantilevered Pergola – *(Fig. 41)*

Cantilevering in this pergola leaves the centre clear of supports and gives plenty of space for access or a central feature. The construction involves the use of both brick and timber although it might be possible to use heavy timber uprights instead of brick if they can be anchored securely. Another alternative, particularly for a large-scale structure, would be reinforced stone columns.

Fig. 41 This cantilevered pergola is unusual in that it requires no central supports, even over quite a wide diameter.

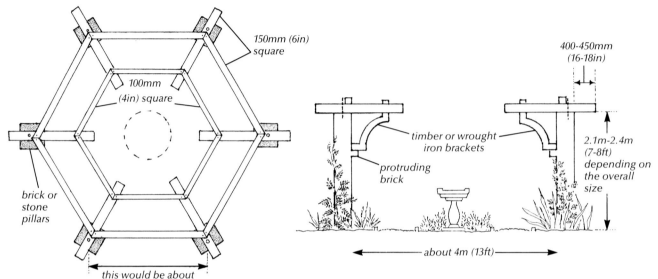

150mm (6in) square

100mm (4in) square

brick or stone pillars

this would be about 2m (6ft 6in) for a pergola diameter of 4m (13ft)

timber or wrought iron brackets

protruding brick

about 4m (13ft)

400-450mm (16-18in)

2.1m-2.4m (7-8ft) depending on the overall size

The brick (or stone) columns must have substantial concrete foundations. A 300 mm (12 in) square pillar should have a deep foundation which is at least 600 mm (24 in) square. The surface of this can, however, be quite deep underground so that there is a good 300 mm (12 in) of soil on top for some planting, although climbing plants should be planted with their roots outside this foundation area. A 'one-and-a-half' brick column (300 mm/12 in square) has a small cavity running through the centre. Steel reinforcing bars can be incorporated in the foundation and brought up through the centre of each column to within one or two courses of the top. These columns should be at least 2.1 m (7 ft) tall and preferably more. A coach bolt is mortared firmly into the cavity right at the top of each column so that it protrudes by about 175 mm (7 in) and can, therefore, take a piece of timber 150 mm (6 in) thick. Before being mortared in, the bolt could be fitted with a washer or two so that, once buried in mortar, these can increase the anchorage. In this particular pergola there are six columns but a larger version could have eight, provided that they do not end up too close together and produce an oppressive mass of brick or stonework.

One brick is left protruding on each column about 700 mm (2 ft 4 in) down from the top, to support a wooden bracket.

Timberwork

Good, heavy beams can be used – 150 mm (6 in) thick for main beams and 100 mm (4 in) thick for subsidiary ones. Main beams are bolted down onto the top of each brick column and are supported by wooden brackets beneath, which rest on the protruding bricks. An alternative to these wooden brackets and protruding bricks could be substantial wrought-iron brackets bolted directly onto the columns. The main beams will be lowered down onto the bolts which have been fixed into the top of the columns. Each beam will, therefore, need a hole at this point. The diameter of this hole should be wider than that of the bolt, resulting in a loose fit. A nut and generous washer on top will hold the beam down but the loose fit will allow some lateral movement as the timber expands and contracts. All other joints must be tight; coach screws would be useful in many instances. Provided that the bolts in the top of each column are completely secure, this pergola should be capable of supporting a good deal of weight despite the absence of a central support.

Plants for pergolas and arches

There is a wide selection of climbers which can be chosen for their attractive foliage, flowers or fragrance. Many of these are described in Chapter 1 (see pages 22–3) but because pergolas are often more exposed than walls, climbers which are not entirely hardy should be avoided unless the climate is relatively mild.

Bridges

Flat bridge – *(Fig. 42a)*

This simple pedestrian bridge is easy to construct, reasonably decorative and could fit into all but the smallest gardens since it has no fixed size.

Foundations

These will depend upon the amount of use the bridge receives. For occasional decorative (normal garden) use, concrete blocks set in the ground, back from the edge of the ditch or stream, should suffice. The fact that the handrail supports go down into the ground either side of the bridge, should prevent it from being dislodged sideways. For heavier use, block concrete foundations would be cast on site, going deep into stable ground either side of the stream/ditch. A heavy duty bolt can be incorporated into the top of each block so that at least 50 mm (2 in) of thread protrudes vertically. Steel brackets are attached to each side of the bridge so that they coincide with the bolt thread in each block. The bridge can then be bolted into position at four

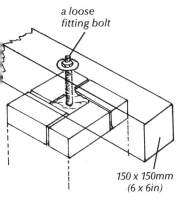

a loose fitting bolt

*150 x 150mm
(6 x 6in)*

Fixing a beam on top of a column.

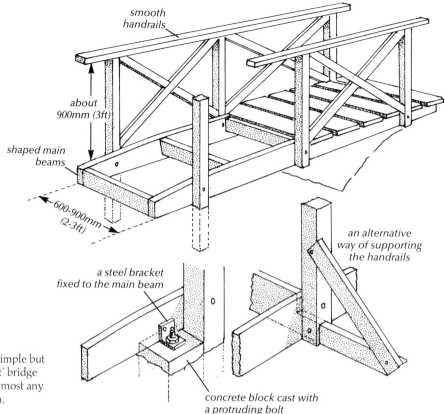

smooth handrails

about 900mm (3ft)

shaped main beams

600-900mm (2-3ft)

a steel bracket fixed to the main beam

an alternative way of supporting the handrails

concrete block cast with a protruding bolt

Fig. 42(a) A simple but attractive 'flat' bridge suitable for almost any size of garden.

locations. Great care is needed to position the foundation bolts so that they coincide precisely with holes in the bridge brackets.

Main structure

This is a frame comprising two main beams (which will span the stream/ditch) and cross beams. The main beams will have to be at least 50 mm (2 in) thick and, depending on length, about 200 mm (8 in) deep before shaping. They should not end up less than 125 mm (5 in) deep after shaping. These figures assume that the overall span will be about 4 m (13 ft). Cross beams might use the same timber but could have smaller dimensions, say 100 mm (4 in) deep and 50 mm (2 in) thick.

The uprights for the handrails will be 75 mm (3 in) or 100 mm (4 in) square. The handrails themselves should be in planed timber (free from splinters) and stout enough for the job. The main frame can be assembled *in situ* or off site but will be heavy to move. Once this has been fixed into position, handrail supports can be added. Those close to either end of the bridge are extended down into the ground before being bolted to the main frame. Others, away from the ends, will end flush with the underside of the frame (and be bolted). If this arrangement does not offer enough rigidity, the cross beams in the main frame may be extended out either side by about 450 mm (18 in) so that a cross brace can be fixed from the end of these onto the handrail supports. On a small bridge this will probably not be necessary and could look cumbersome. Handrails are then screwed into position together with any timber infilling. Finally, the flooring slats are nailed or screwed (with expansion gaps), overlapping each side by at least 150 mm (6 in).

The overall width of the bridge could be anything between 600–900 mm (24–36 in) although large bridges may need a greater width and heavier timber to retain good proportions.

If any form of staining is to take place, take care not to spill or drip any into the stream.

Curved bridge – *(Fig. 42b)*

(**b**) This curved bridge is more complex to build than the flat one and is less suitable for very small gardens.

An alternative to the 'flat' bridge is this curved and slightly more ornate version. It does, however, need to be a reasonable length so that its shape can be developed properly. This may make it less suited to very small gardens.

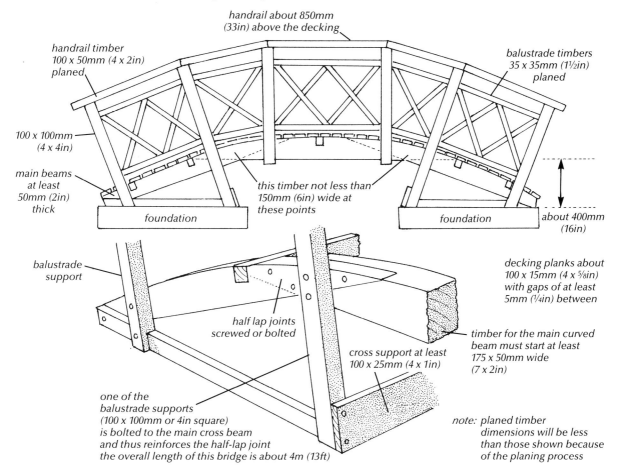

handrail about 850mm (33in) above the decking

handrail timber 100 x 50mm (4 x 2in) planed

balustrade timbers 35 x 35mm (1½in) planed

100 x 100mm (4 x 4in)

main beams at least 50mm (2in) thick

foundation

this timber not less than 150mm (6in) wide at these points

foundation

about 400mm (16in)

balustrade support

half lap joints screwed or bolted

decking planks about 100 x 15mm (4 x ⅝in) with gaps of at least 5mm (¼in) between

cross support at least 100 x 25mm (4 x 1in)

timber for the main curved beam must start at least 175 x 50mm wide (7 x 2in)

one of the balustrade supports (100 x 100mm or 4in square) is bolted to the main cross beam and thus reinforces the half-lap joint the overall length of this bridge is about 4m (13ft)

note: planed timber dimensions will be less than those shown because of the planing process

Chapter 8

Garden Buildings

The dimensions suggested for the following structures could easily be changed to suit your own special needs. There will come a point, however, where larger spans will need greater support by increasing timber thickness or by using an alternative method of construction. Conversely, where dimensions are significantly smaller, thinner timber and possibly simpler construction techniques could be employed.

Dimensions of frame timbers are given under individual projects but it must be remembered that pressure treated or sprayed timber should be used throughout.

Cladding materials

The choice of cladding will depend very much on the following:

(*i*) appearance and general effect
(*ii*) durability and weatherproof qualities
(*iii*) suitability for the shape and type of structure
(*iv*) cost.

Here are some of the more readily available materials. I have assumed that all these will be used on *vertical* surfaces and not for roofing (which is discussed on pages 103–4).

FEATHEREDGE BOARDING Apart from 100 mm (4 in) wide oak boards which may be used vertically for closeboard fencing, most is softwood which can be bought ready pressure treated. Other available widths include 125 mm (5 in) and 150 mm (6 in). When calculating your requirements it is important to remember that each plank should overlap the one below by at least 12 mm (½ in) and preferably more, especially if the boards are still wet from pressure treatment as they are likely to shrink while drying out. Each board is tapered, having one thick edge and one thinner one. The boards are nailed horizontally so that the thick edges overlap the thin ones to produce a weatherproof finish.

This type of boarding is relatively inexpensive compared with most others and looks reasonably attractive. It is nearly always 'sawn' so is seldom smooth. Once treated with a weather repellant paint or stain, it is quite weatherproof.

An attractive, two-storey timber playhouse like this will fit into any reasonable sized garden and keep the children occupied for hours.

WANEY-EDGED ELM   Not necessarily from elm trees, this describes planks which have one wavy edge (often still with bark on) and one sawn edge. It is overlapped horizontally in a similar way to feather-edge boarding, but because of its uneven edge, may require a greater degree of overlap. Widths vary and often average 200 mm (8 in) or so, but its thickness tends to remain the same across the board, with no significant tapering. It therefore overlaps in a slightly clumsy way to produce a more rustic effect. Its weathering properties are similar to those of feather-edge boarding.

SHIP-LAP BOARDING   This is a profiled board or plank, usually in softwood with widths of 125 mm (5 in) or 150 mm (6 in). The bottom edge is shaped or rebated so that it fits horizontally and snugly onto the top edge of the plank below. This produces a smooth and completely sealed surface on the inside but an attractive profiled weatherproof exterior. These boards should never be nailed wet, otherwise they will shrink on drying out to leave gaps, through which driving rain could penetrate. The profiling of these boards leaves them with a smooth, planed surface which takes stain very well.

TONGUE AND GROOVE BOARDING   There are many styles of profile available for both interior and exterior tongue and groove cladding. Although mostly softwood, some boarding is available in cedar and other resilient timbers. Its name is derived from the fact that a thin tongue all down one side locates into a groove on the other to produce an interlocking weathertight cladding. It is not, however, designed to repel rain in a horizontal plane and is best used as vertical cladding. Like ship-lap, it is planed smooth. It needs thoroughly treating with preservative because moisture will often hang around between the tongue and groove. Staining is more satisfactory than painting or varnishing.

SHEET MATERIALS   The most widely used of these is exterior grade plywood, available in a wide choice of thicknesses. The thicker the board, the less frequent the frame timbers need be, but even relatively thin boards remain quite rigid on widely spaced frames. This boarding seldom looks as attractive as the various types of horizontal cladding but can be stained and could be decorated by additional pieces of timber which might be used to produce a pattern in a contrasting colour. Half logs can also be fixed onto plywood to produce an attractive, weatherproof log cabin effect.

COMPOSITE BOARDS   There are a number of different boards available which have been produced from wood chips or flakes brought together under great pressure and bonded with weather-resistant adhesives. The majority are about 1 cm (3/8 in) thick and are not particularly attractive. They are, however, relatively inexpensive and, if used cunningly, can be made to look quite acceptable.

CORRUGATED SHEET   See under 'Roofing materials', below.

Roofing materials

Apart from various types of tiles, the following products are widely used for the roofs of garden buildings, mainly because they are relatively light in weight, easy to install and often inexpensive.

MINERAL ROOFING FELT   This is a thick grade of bitumastic felt with a dressing of green, black or even red grit. It must be fully supported by a sheet of ply or composite board. Felt is bought as rolls and is laid horizontally with at least 50 mm (2 in) overlaps. Although it can be nailed onto vertical surfaces around the outside edges of a roof, it must be stuck down onto the roof itself (with a special bitumastic adhesive). It is quite easy to use and may last in excess of 10 years before needing replacement. Alternatively, horizontal strips of mock, felt tiles are available, together with special ridge and edging pieces to produce a 'tiled' roof. Although the overall effect is far more attractive than that obtained with plain rolls of felt, it is usually more expensive.

CORRUGATED SHEETING   All these must be supported on fairly frequent cross beams and be given a pronounced slope. Each sheet should overlap the next by at least one corrugation and the end of one sheet must overlap the beginning of the next by at least 75 mm (3 in). Where sheets are not given a steep slope, this overlap should be increased to discourage water from seeping back and leaking. All corrugated sheets are fixed with long screws or nails which enter the ridges (not the troughs) and pass down into the beam below. These fixings must have quite close spacing otherwise the wind will get under the sheets and lift them.

CORRUGATED FIBRE SHEET   This is made from bitumen-impregnated fibres compressed into a thin but strong and durable lightweight corrugated sheet. Each sheet is usually about 90 cm (3 ft) wide and 1.8 m (6 ft) long. Ridge pieces and various other components are used to finish off the roof and this material is available in black, green and sometimes dull red. It can be cut with a fine-toothed saw and fixing nails can be simply banged through the ridges.

CORRUGATED PVC   This clear corrugated sheet is quite strong but will deteriorate in the presence of strong sunlight so may have a life of only a few years. To compensate, it is relatively inexpensive. This sheeting is best worked when the air is warm – under cold conditions it may be brittle. It can be cut with scissors but these should be used in a series of short cutting movements, never allowing the blades to close and complete a cut. If they do, the sheet may split.

Other types of corrugated sheet may be available, including

fibreglass which is not perfectly clear (opaque) but will last many years and is very tough.

FLAT SHEETS   The two main products in use are acrylic and polycarbonate.

Acrylic sheeting   This is a thin, flexible but crystal clear sheet which does not seem to deteriorate in the presence of sunlight. It may, however, gradually become brittle. Because it is so flexible, it will need frequent supports in both directions. Fixings must be of a type which will not leak – not easy to achieve on a flat sheet. Special slotted plastic strips may be available to join sheets down either side but these often have to be used in conjunction with some form of weatherproof mastic. Acrylic sheeting is best used only on very steep slopes (pitches) or vertically as windows. The sheets can be cut with a laminate cutter which scores a deep groove through the material. A narrow strip of wood can then be placed beneath the groove, and the sheet snapped in half by pressing down on both sides of the wood – in a similar manner to cutting glass.

Polycarbonate sheeting   This is available mainly as a twin-walled, reinforced, semi-transparent sheet. It is possible to see through it, but not clearly. It is very strong, slightly flexible and comes in large sheets which can be joined using special fixings. It has excellent insulation properties (being used widely in conservatory construction), is not affected by sunlight but is very expensive. Fixings must be made carefully to ensure there are no leaks and cutting can be done with a fine-toothed saw.

FEATHER-EDGE BOARDING   can also be used (horizontally) on steeply sloping roofs but will only be weathertight with a roofing felt underneath and a water repellent stain or preservative.

The Playhouse – *(Fig. 43)*

This is a two-storey, sectional building. Although it could be made larger than suggested here, it should never be made taller without increasing both width and depth in proportion. If this is not done it is just possible that the weight of two children playing upstairs could rock the house.

Floor

This is a simple square frame of 100 mm × 50 mm (4 in × 2 in) sawn timber with one cross beam and a covering of timber floorboards or a sheet of weather-resistant ply (not less than 1 cm or ⅜ in thick). It should be mounted, perfectly level, on bricks set in the ground, with pieces of felt or plastic damp proofing between the bricks and the timber.

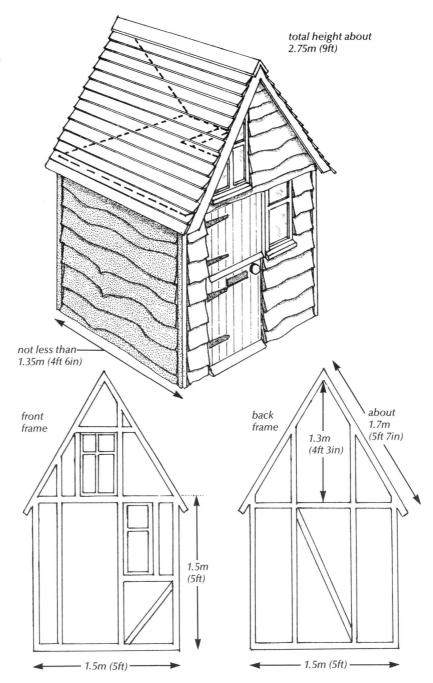

Fig 43 A traditionally styled playhouse with an upstairs but which is still sufficiently compact for all but the smallest gardens.

total height about
2.75m (9ft)

not less than 1.35m (4ft 6in)

front frame

back frame

1.3m (4ft 3in)

about 1.7m (5ft 7in)

1.5m (5ft)

1.5m (5ft)

1.5m (5ft)

Sides

These are two identical rectangular frames made from 50 mm × 50 mm (2 in × 2 in) sawn timber and should be made 100 mm (4 in) narrower than the floor so that there is room on the floor for the front and back frames too. Cladding can be horizontal feather-edge, ship-lap or waney-edged elm boarding, made flush down either side and along the top but extended down below the bottom of the frame by as much as possible so that the weather is kept away from the floor section. The weatherproof qualities of all the sections can be significantly improved by stretching building paper, thin bitumastic felt or thick PVC sheeting across the frames before cladding is nailed into place.

Back

The frame uses the same timber as the sides and has two intermediate vertical supports. On a significantly larger version, an intermediate horizontal support would also be necessary. Cladding of both the back and the front is best done after all four 'sides' have been fixed together and onto the base with long screws.

Front section

This must be identical in size and shape to the back but, of course, will have additional framework for windows and a door. Again, the cladding is best done later after assembly.

Cladding

Once all four sides have been screwed together, the front and back can be clad. This cladding should extend across the sawn ends of the side cladding to produce a reasonably neat and weathertight joint. If necessary an extra board can be fixed all round the bottom but this must, of course, be overlapped by the one above it.

Roof

Irrespective of which material is used for the actual roof cladding, the two panels should start as single sheets of all weather ply (not less than about 5 mm or ³⁄₁₆ in thick). These sheets should be large enough to provide generously overhanging eaves all round. With the main house frame fixed together and clad, one sheet of ply can be positioned on one sloping side so that its top edge coincides with the apex, the front edge overlaps by at least 150 mm (6 in) and the back by a little less. It can then, very temporarily, be tacked into position so that a line can be drawn (inside) tight up against the sloping frame of the front and back sections – beginning at the apex and ending level with the top of the side section. The sheet is then removed and two strips of timber (50 mm × 50 mm or 2 in × 2 in) fixed securely on the inside of these two lines. This will mean that when the roof sheet is replaced, the two strips should fit snugly between the front and back sections and on the top bar of the side. Two more strips can be added right down the front and back edges, in readiness to hold the gables or eave boards. Feather-edge boarding used on the roof will have to be nailed, so a layer of felt or P V C can be laid underneath for extra weatherproofing. This boarding must project far enough beyond the two edging strips of 50 mm × 50 mm (2 in × 2 in) to accommodate and overhang the eaves. The roof can be finally held down with screws inside and a ridge of timber fixed on top – preferably with screws so that it can be removed should the house need dismantling and moving elsewhere at a later date.

Windows

The easiest way to finish the (non-opening) windows is to attach a piece of timber all round the inside of the basic frame leaving something like a 15 mm (½ in) rebate on the front. At the same time a piece of windowsill can be fixed into the bottom of each window frame. Once any treatment or staining has been completed, a piece of acrylic can be fixed in, bedded on mastic and held with strips of 'L'-shaped plastic beading tacked with copper pins. Any divisions within the windows will be made afterwards by simply making up a cross of thin timber and fixing it onto the outside of the acrylic window pane.

Top floor

This will only span about three quarters of the area since access space has to be left for stairs. The simplest construction is to use stout ply on a basic frame and support it on strong brackets attached to the house frame, as close to the roof pitch as possible. A small ladder can be used as stairs but should be fixed so that it cannot be removed!

Door

Again, a simple frame (or frames) clad with a suitable style of boarding can be hung using heavy duty hinges. A letterbox, door bell, handle and even a small window can all be added for extra character.

The inside can be boarded out, painted and have curtains hung at the windows. The outside can be made attractive by using perhaps two contrasting colours of stain rather than just brown. Do not use paint since it is bound to deteriorate. Further refinements could include battery lighting, a smoke detector alarm, hanging baskets and a window box.

Following page – inset picture: Though modern, this 'Victorian' summerhouse is similar to the rustic version shown in Fig. 44.

Main picture: Here is an impressive focal point for any large garden.

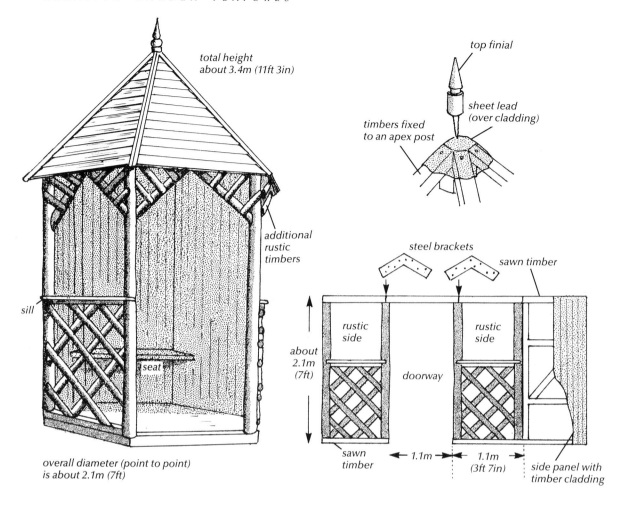

total height
about 3.4m (11ft 3in)

top finial

sheet lead
(over cladding)

timbers fixed
to an apex post

additional
rustic
timbers

steel brackets

sawn timber

sill

rustic
side

rustic
side

about
2.1m
(7ft)

doorway

seat

sawn
timber

1.1m

1.1m
(3ft 7in)

side panel with
timber cladding

overall diameter (point to point)
is about 2.1m (7ft)

'Victorian' Summerhouse – *(Fig. 44)*

Fig. 44 A Victorian summerhouse copied from one designed in about 1880.

Because of its shape, this project requires some careful construction and although it is a copy of a summerhouse designed around 1884, various aspects have been modified so that it can be built partly from modern, pressure treated timbers. Overall, however, the effect must be rustic. Some parts of the construction are sectional but the finished summerhouse cannot be easily dismantled or moved.

Floor

This is a hexagonal frame of timber with at least two cross beams. The timber should not be less than 50 mm × 75 mm (2 in × 3 in) thick and be well supported on bricks below. Rather than using any complex joints, the frame can be held together quite easily with metal truss plates (used on both sides of each joint). A traditional flooring of floor 'boards' is more appropriate than marine ply or any other sheet material. The floor must be set perfectly level.

Panelled sides

There are three of these. The simple frames could be made from timber measuring 50 mm × 50 mm (2 in × 2 in) or 50 mm × 75 mm (2 in × 3 in) and have sufficient cross members to support the relatively thin, vertical strips of pine panelling. The frames are fixed to the floor, then to each other and finally linked across the top corners with relatively inconspicuous metal plates before pine panelling is nailed front and back. Cedar panelling could be used but will appear less traditional. It would be prudent to use a weathertight lining material beneath the outer panelling and to treat thoroughly all the panelling with a preservative since it is highly vulnerable to decay.

Rustic sides

The two rustic sides combine the use of rustic poles (with the bark removed) and sawn timber. It is best to build these as self-contained panels, then fix them into position afterwards.

Doorway

This remaining gap requires only a sawn timber beam across the top, securely fixed to each rustic panel (perhaps using metal plates) and some rustic corner bracing to match that on the rustic sides.

Roof

This is the most difficult part and is built *in situ*. There are two possible techniques: the first is traditional and ideal for all sizes of summer-house.

METHOD 1   Six beams with an angled top surface will be brought together at the top by a short, stout, six-sided apex post. These beams will need to be about 50 mm wide and 35 mm thick (2 in × 1 ½ in) – thick enough, in fact, not to give when roof cladding is being nailed on. The apex post must have six sides which are wide enough to accept the end of each beam. These will be secured with long screws. The other (lower) end of each beam will be notched to fit over the side sections and provide a short overhang. If feather-edge cladding is used, it can be made more weatherproof with a bitumastic underfelt. The cladding is cut and nailed into position, over the felt, starting at the bottom with the first board overhanging the sides, to produce 'eaves'. The final, topmost pieces will be very small and should be drilled before nailing to prevent splitting. The six ridges which are formed by the joint between each roof segment can be finished off with shaped wooden strips (or with narrow strips of lead). Since the apex post does not extend above the roof (as it might appear) a small piece of lead (or similar material) can be used to cap the very top of the roof. A ball or ornamental spike (finial), complete with a protruding screw thread (and some mastic), can then be screwed down through this 'cap' into the top of the apex post to complete the roof.

METHOD 2   This is less traditional, better suited to the smaller versions of the summerhouse and simpler than the first method. It is possible to make the hexagonal roof cone from six identical triangles of stout marine ply. Before these are brought together and joined with brackets (or even hinges), cladding is nailed onto the outside of each segment (again with an underfelt). The clad cone can then be lowered onto the main structure and fixed down, probably with steel straps or brackets. The triangles must be large enough to produce a cone that will overhang the sides and form eaves. The joints between sections of cladding and the top can be finished off as before but it may prove a little more difficult to fit a finial without an apex post.

Inside

Bench seats can be fitted against the three-panelled sides or they can be omitted in favour of garden furniture. The whole structure can be stained or left 'natural'. Shrubs may be used to conceal the back part of the summerhouse partially and climbers trained against the rustic posts either side of the doorway (preferably not very thorny climbing roses).

Hanging Bird Table – *(Fig. 45)*

This table is cunningly designed to cause difficulty for greedy birds like pigeons, jays, magpies and so on, in favour of the smaller species. It could also give squirrels quite a challenge. There are two triangular frames made from planed timber (measuring 25 mm or 30 mm square, 1 in or 1¼ in square) – large enough, in fact, for small 'half lap' joints.

Set within this frame is a series of wooden poles or rods (these could be square rather than round). Their distance apart will decide which birds can pass through and which cannot. If squirrels are a problem and wooden bars are likely to be chewed, then tubular steel can be used instead. At the top of these two frames is a small triangle of thin ply, made slightly larger than the frame itself and which will help to support the detachable section of roof. The two frames are fixed to a solid timber or marine ply base (not less than 10 mm or ⅜ in thick) just 'in' a little way from each end so that a portion of the table is accessible to some larger birds.

About three quarters of the roof is in the form of two marine ply sheets (not less than 5 mm or ¼ in thick) fixed to the two triangular frames, as far up as the bottom of the two small ply triangles. Exterior adhesive and pins (or screws) can be used for fixing. A small bar may also be fixed across each end of the table to help prevent food from falling off. The top, removable section of the roof must be large enough to overhang the lower sections by about 10 mm (⅜ in). Since the marine ply from which it is made will be relatively thin, some wooden fixing blocks will have to be used inside the apex. Thin wire (or polypropylene string) is fixed into the top of each triangular frame and threaded through two holes in the removable top section before ending up around a tree branch or some other suitable hanging point. Food can be placed in the main body of the table by moving the top section of the roof up the wires.

Although this table is illustrated in plain wood it could, with a little effort, be laminated with straight twigs, thatch, split cane or even roofing felt cut into small tiles.

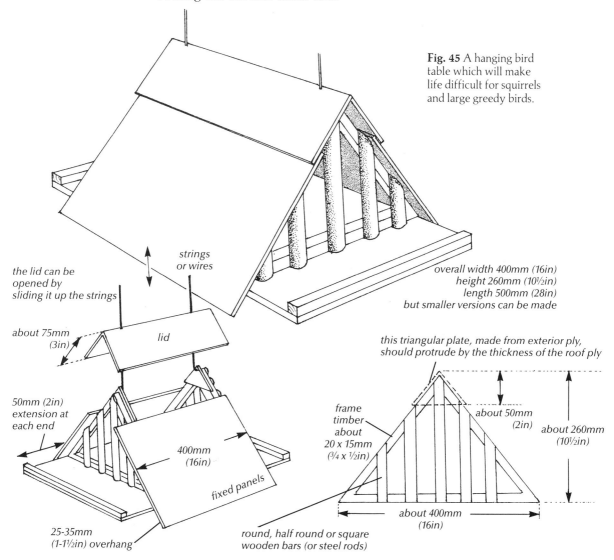

Fig. 45 A hanging bird table which will make life difficult for squirrels and large greedy birds.

strings or wires

the lid can be opened by sliding it up the strings

overall width 400mm (16in)
height 260mm (10½in)
length 500mm (28in)
but smaller versions can be made

about 75mm (3in)

lid

this triangular plate, made from exterior ply, should protrude by the thickness of the roof ply

50mm (2in) extension at each end

about 50mm (2in)

about 260mm (10½in)

frame timber about 20 x 15mm (¾ x ½in)

400mm (16in)

fixed panels

25-35mm (1-1½in) overhang

round, half round or square wooden bars (or steel rods)

about 400mm (16in)

Pavilion Bird Table – *(Fig. 46)*

This is more traditional with its ground support and its open access. The roof looks complicated but is remarkably simple to construct. Although the shape and dimensions of each section are given, any slight variation will result in a slightly different roof shape. The sections labelled (*i*) are best cut from a plank of wood – not ply – at least 20 mm (¾ in) thick. The sections (*ii*) would be marine ply not thinner than 5 mm (¼ in). These four pieces must be screwed (and possibly glued) together before the rest of the roof is measured and cut to fit. Often it can be helpful to make some sections in cardboard

Fig. 46 A traditional style of bird table with an attractive roof which could be thatched or tiled with roofing felt.

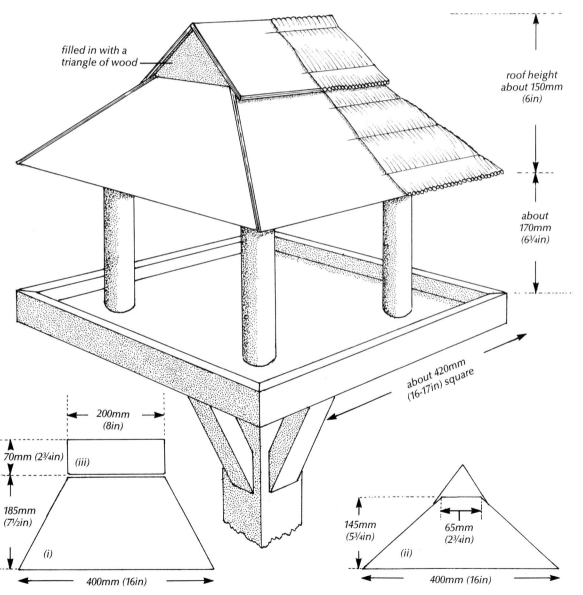

114

first, try them and modify as necessary, before finally cutting out a shape in wood. This could well apply to the sections (*iii*) and the two triangular end plates which will help to hold them together. Ideally the two sections labelled (*i*) should reach a little way into the top section of the roof so that these two small triangular end plates can make a weatherproof union. The top section of the roof can be fixed down with the help of internal fixing blocks. Two fairly thick wooden bars will also be needed, running along the underside of the roof into which the four pillars can be fixed.

The table itself must be made from a sheet of timber or marine ply which is at least 20 mm (¾ in) thick. Four holes are drilled to take the four pillars and an upstanding edge pinned all around the outside. The four angled braces coming up from the stand must avoid these four pillar positions so that any fixing screws have an unimpeded passage. In sequence, the table platform and stand should be assembled before the pillars are fixed in and the roof is fixed on.

Once again, the roof could be laminated with a range of materials to give this bird table some additional charm.

Garden Work Shed – *(Fig. 47)*

Most garden sheds are just somewhere to put the tools or the garden chairs. This one combines some additional features with an interesting design. The actual 'shed' section is more like a very large cupboard with its doors opening out into a covered area. One obvious advantage of this is that it allows tools to be cleaned and put away without interruption from rain or snow. Opposite the shed doors is a space which can either be used to store logs (or anything else) or into which a bench can be fitted for potting, seed sowing and so on. Although this project is more suitable for larger gardens, it is designed to be as unobtrusive as possible, especially when planted around with some shrubs. Only one entrance is apparent in the sketch, suggesting that the opposite end is solid, but there could be an entrance at both ends. This might provide access to another part of the garden so that the 'shed' acts as a sort of archway or perhaps an entrance to a fruit and vegetable garden.

The dimensions shown could be varied somewhat although the overall design is controlled, to some extent, by the height of the doorway which really could not be much smaller than is shown here. The structure could be lengthened but this would mean having an extra 'end' frame fitted through the centre for additional support.

Foundations

Rows of hollow 225 mm (9 in) concrete blocks are set perfectly level into firm ground and positioned to coincide with the main framework. Strips of damp proof material must be placed between

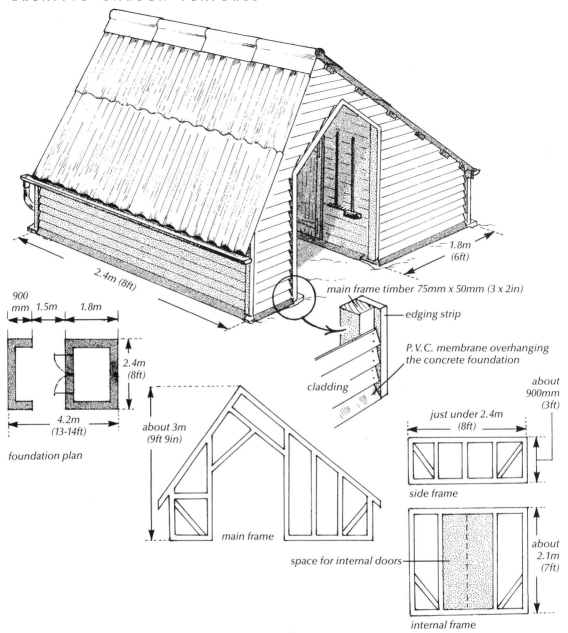

900 mm · 1.5m · 1.8m

4.2m (13-14ft)

2.4m (8ft)

foundation plan

2.4m (8ft)

1.8m (6ft)

about 3m (9ft 9in)

main frame

main frame timber 75mm x 50mm (3 x 2in)

edging strip

P.V.C. membrane overhanging the concrete foundation

cladding

just under 2.4m (8ft)

about 900mm (3ft)

side frame

space for internal doors

about 2.1m (7ft)

internal frame

Fig. 47 This compact work shed has been designed for the larger garden where tool storage, under cover work space and log storage are required under one roof.

the timber frame and the surface of these blocks. Steel pins can be driven down inside some of the blocks, leaving a spur above onto which the frame can be screwed or bolted for stability.

Main end frames

There must be two of these. Their design will vary depending on whether they are to be open-ended or 'solid'. However, they must both have exactly the same overall shape. The timber used should be sawn and tanalized and be not less than 75 mm × 50 mm (3 in × 2 in).

In districts which experience heavy snow, or for sheds which are larger than the one suggested here, timber measuring 100 mm × 50 mm (4 in × 2 in) would be a better choice. Since these frames will be clad with boarding, for the most part they must be flush. This can be achieved by using half-lap or better still, mortice and tennon joints except for angled braces which can more easily be fixed inside the main frame with nails. Elsewhere screws are used.

In districts prone to strong winds, extra cross braces can be incorporated here and there although the basic structure should be quite strong in the form shown.

Roof beams

One of the best materials for this type of roof is corrugated fibre board, perhaps interspersed with the odd sheet of corrugated PVC for extra light. This has to be fixed onto horizontal cross beams which are spaced no further apart than 900 mm (3 ft). These beams will form a major part of the building frame so should not be less than 100 mm × 50 mm (4 in × 2 in) and, as suggested in the sketch, not longer than 2.4 m (8 ft) without an additional, centre support frame. The end sections must be propped up on their foundations while the cross beams are gradually nailed into position (using ring-shanked nails). These beams will have to be long enough to overhang the end frames by about 75 mm (3 in). Once they have been nailed on, the building can stand up on its own but will not be rigid.

Side frames

Two side frames made from timber not less than 75 mm × 50 mm (3 in × 2 in) along with the interior door frame section can now be fixed between the two ends (with nails). Once these are in position, the structure should be quite rigid.

Roof cladding

The corrugated fibre board is ideal because it is strong, lightweight and easy to fix. Almost any other type of roofing could be used, including tiles but, for these, the timber support layout would have to be changed and additional support becomes necessary.

A roof of this size will shed a lot of rainwater. This could be collected in tanks although the potential gutter line is very low, making the collection of water more difficult than from higher, more conventional eaves. Nevertheless, the rainwater ought to be collected in a gutter and guided away from the foundations and the immediate vicinity of the structure. Two soffit boards are fixed across the extended ends of the main frames so that a gutter can be used. These boards need to be at least 25 mm (1 in) thick and about 150 mm (6 in) wide so that they will not bow or warp between the frames. The roof cladding extends just beyond these boards to a point where rainwater will run cleanly into the gutters. The roof cladding must also overhang both the front and rear sections/frames by at least 75 mm (3 in).

Cladding the sides

Most types of cladding have to begin at the bottom. In this building the cladding might have to start very close to the ground unless the foundation blocks have been elevated in some way. To help with weatherproofing and as protection from splashing rain, a wide strip of PVC or felt damp proofing should be fixed across the bottom of the frame so that it extends below the top of the foundation. This will prevent any water from flowing back under the frame. The bottom cladding board is then fixed over this, leaving some of the strip protruding from the bottom edge. Boards will have to be carefully measured and cut to fit under the roofing overhang, around the protruding roof beams and around the open doorway. If logs are to be stored in the area opposite the internal doors, the cladding could be left off that side for better air circulation. The frame containing the internal door(s) can be clad in the same material or something different. Hooks could be fixed into the small blank panels either side for hanging tools, coats etc. The floor can be paved (on top of a sheet of PVC) or left as soil.

Lighting and power sockets would be a useful addition, opening up the possibility of using power tools and re-charging a hedge trimmer or whatever.

In windy gardens, the open entrance should perhaps face a sheltered direction although, on the whole this design means that the structure is remarkably weather resistant.

The cladding could be stained almost any colour. One possibility is to have black roof sheets and green cladding, while another is green roof sheets and brown or possibly greyish cladding. A wide range of stains is always available at a specialist decorator's merchant.

Chapter 9

Garden Illusions, Themes and Lighting

Illusions

Fig. 48 This flat, wall-mounted trellis will help to give a small garden an illusion of space.

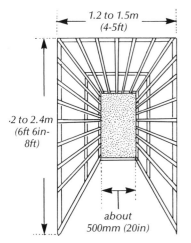

1.2 to 1.5m
(4-5ft)

·2 to 2.4m
(6ft 6in-
8ft)

about
500mm (20in)

Although this trellis would normally employ timber laths the same width throughout, extra effort spent on tapering laths so that they narrow towards the centre will produce a more convincing effect.

No illusion is easy to create in a garden because there are so many outside influences interfering with the effect and making it less convincing. There are, however, ways of at least partially falsifying perspective, of making certain areas appear larger, nearer or further away and some other interesting ideas which help to add just a small touch of genius here and there.

Perspective wall trellis – *(Fig. 48)*

Thorough research, attention to detail and careful construction can, in certain instances, go quite a long way in fooling the eye. The illusion has to be based on the acceptance that objects and detail appear smaller, the further away they are.

The first example uses a wall trellis which has been very carefully made so that the gaps between cross members become closer towards the centre and the cross members themselves taper in width. The central area of the trellis therefore appears furthest away. The wall within the central area ought to be virtually textureless – perhaps rendered so that tell-tale rows of bricks or a rough surface do not give the game away too quickly. A plain dark background works well. Any planting will have to complement the illusion by displaying smaller leaves at the back and larger ones to the fore. This can make the choice of plants difficult. The most convincing approach is to use the same type of plant throughout but have cultivars with different leaf sizes – bamboos are a good example. If there is an artist available, a dark background could be bettered by a mural of sky and clouds.

On a larger scale, perspective can be falsified by making paths narrow as they go further away. Hedges can be made progressively shorter and trees smaller. It has to be remembered, though, that everything would look most odd if viewed from the opposite direction. Even colours have a part to play, with blues and greys tending to appear further from the eye than red and orange.

Mirrors

The use of mirrors can, if framed in some way and positioned carefully, extend an otherwise small garden or give the impression of another area laying beyond a gate or hole in the wall. It is important to position the mirror so that it is not possible to see yourself while viewing from a vantage point.

Mirrors are most convincing when fitted into an archway or into a space in a wall, especially if it is feasible that more garden could exist beyond (it might be hard to believe if the mirror is fixed to a garage wall!). Tall narrow mirrors, perhaps down to the ground, often provide the best illusion but the bottom half of any such mirror will quickly become dirty and need regular cleaning. A bed of cobbles or stones would help to minimize this, as would some planting.

The mirror must be weatherproofed in some way or it will soon deteriorate. One technique I have seen used is to seal all the edges with all-weather, clear adhesive tape, then paint the back (silvered) surface with a suitable paint or varnish. A small test on a piece of mirror should be carried out to check that the paint or varnish will not damage or blister the silvering. This weatherproofing is obviously especially important on mirrors which reach the ground.

More than one mirror set at different angles within a relatively small area can produce some interesting effects.

Invisible gates and doors

Gates which are in use but need disguising could simply have climbing plants trained on them. These plants will quite happily hinge with the gate. It is better to choose plants which are not self clinging so that they can be removed when the gate needs renovating. On small gates, honeysuckle is ideal but larger five-bar gates will accommodate plants like climbing roses, clematis and *Vitis coignetiae*.

One idea which I have seen took the idea a stage further (Fig. 49). A stone house had quite a large integral garage but the owners did not want the garage doors to spoil the general character of the building. The space occupied by the garage doors was divided not in half but into one third and two thirds. The one third was in the form of a typical cottage style wooden door with a latch. The two thirds

Fig. 49 Garage doors cleverly disguised, with the help of some artwork, to look like the rest of the house.

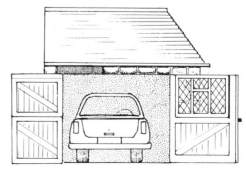

portion was one large door which had a window that matched the other downstairs windows and stonewalling painted onto the space all round it, once again matching the house. To complete the picture, a climbing rose had been trained across the top of the window so that it would hinge open with everything else. There were even curtains hanging at the window so that when the garage was closed it looked exactly like part of the house. A similar approach could easily be adopted for other situations – garden gates, a mower shed and so on.

Knot and Herb Gardens

The original idea for knot gardens was for these to represent patterns created by ropes curled or 'knotted' on the ground. Over the years, a wide variety of both plant and 'hard' materials have been used to achieve this. At one time, box hedges (*Buxus sempervirens*) were used to separate areas of coloured gravel from shingle or hoggin paths, with no other plants being involved. Lavender is sometimes used instead of box but, on the whole, cannot be clipped to quite the same precision. Specific types or groups of plants are often featured in a knot garden. A planting scheme could be based on annuals or seasonal flowers, including bulbs. Roses are another possibility but are often too vigorous for the limited space available. Herbs are one of the most popular types of plant but the very tallest, like fennel and angelica, may have to be omitted. A symmetrical layout can often be enhanced by the symmetrical use of colour, shape and texture in plants but can be seriously disrupted by any overhanging branches of a nearby tree. Knot and herb gardens should always be sited well away from trees.

The herb garden shown in Fig. 50 would have to be at least 4 m (13 ft) across so that paths could be no less than 450 mm (18 in) wide and the planting spaces a useful size. The outer edging and dividers are likely to be brick (or possibly timber) while paths can either be gravel edged in brick or timber or be entirely of (stock) bricks.

Fig. 50 A geometrical herb garden with brick or brick edged paths and a central ornament.

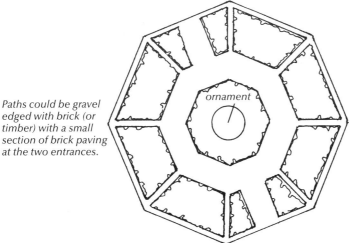

Paths could be gravel edged with brick (or timber) with a small section of brick paving at the two entrances.

ornament

Although only two access points are shown here, a large scale version of this garden could be adapted to have four such points. If the herb (or knot) garden is in an area of grass, all brickwork and edging must be flush for easy mowing. Where paths are gravel, these access points should be hard paved (e.g. brick) so that the gravel is kept away from the grass. It might be appropriate to plant chamomile into the surrounding lawn so that the herb theme can spread beyond the strict limits of the geometric layout, but if this is to be successful, mowing must not be too close (short) and certainly not as close as it would be for a general garden lawn area.

 The two knot gardens illustrated (Figs. 51 and 52) are based on an elliptical island bed which might be in lawn or in the centre of a driveway. In Fig. 51 some areas of planting are not entirely surrounded by box hedges whereas in Fig. 52 they are. Paths are again best laid as shingle or hoggin edged with brick, timber or even 'rope' edging tiles. The narrowness and intricacy of the paths makes grass unsuitable in all but quite large layouts.

With a central ornament and medium-sized herbs this herb garden would soon soften and mature.

Potager

This is a similar concept to the 'knot' but features vegetables. It does, however, have to be a little more practical in layout than a 'knot' because vegetables often need more regular tending and harvesting. To this end, the spaces created by hedges should be a little less intricate, somewhat larger and be based on a pattern which incorporates more straight lines and fewer tight curves.

Fig. 51 A knot garden based on a circular theme with fairly generous areas of gravel or shingle.

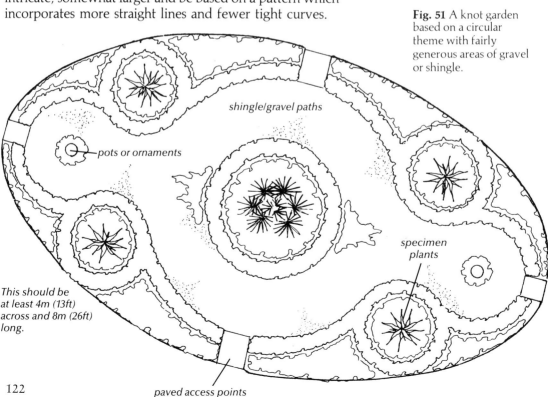

shingle/gravel paths

pots or ornaments

specimen plants

This should be at least 4m (13ft) across and 8m (26ft) long.

paved access points

Rose Garden

There can be similarities between the layout of this and a knot garden but, generally, paths are wider and often of grass. The beds are more generous because roses need more space and must be planted back from the edges of beds so that passers-by do not become hitched on the thorns. Quite elaborate designs can still be used: I once saw a design which had been taken from the pattern on a piece of material.

As with knot gardens, colour themes help to enhance the effect, but coupled with this must be a careful choice of heights since different cultivars can vary so much.

Good soil preparation is essential for a rose garden, where heavier soils produce the best results. Lighter soils can be improved by being double dug and having manure incorporated as deep under the surface as possible. Fungal diseases, especially 'black spot' and 'rose mildew' can be a real problem in low-lying gardens where the air stagnates. This can be partly overcome with the use of more resistant cultivars.

Preserving the shapes

Fig. 52 A knot garden with an angular layout creating more intricate beds and paths than the previous example.

In light soils, constant edging of the grass paths may gradually erode away and blur the original design. One of the best solutions is to use a concealed timber edge just beneath the turf. If this is installed around the edge of existing grass, turves will have to be peeled back so that the timber can be fixed in position. After backfilling with soil, the turves can be put back, ending up on top of the timber. The technique used for this edging is described on page 50.

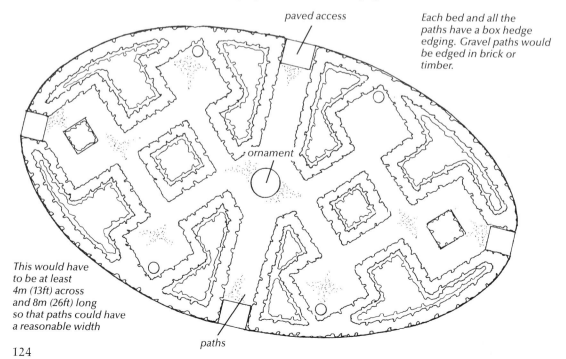

paved access

Each bed and all the paths have a box hedge edging. Gravel paths would be edged in brick or timber.

ornament

This would have to be at least 4m (13ft) across and 8m (26ft) long so that paths could have a reasonable width

paths

Lighting

There are three main approaches to lighting in the garden:

    (*i*) full floodlighting
   (*ii*) low level white light
  (*iii*) coloured lighting.

Full floodlighting

This is usually provided by halogen lamps in the range of 250–500 watts, although other types of lamp are available which can be more economical but not produce a white light. The units are mounted quite high, often on the walls of buildings, and obviously light up a large area. This means that certain parts of the garden (more usually the patio, paths and driveway) are fully lit to allow unhindered activity but not much 'atmosphere'.

Low-level lighting

This can mean 'low' in terms of brilliance, position and voltage. There are many types of fittings available:

    (*i*) short bollards (up to about 1 m or 3 ft 3 in)
   (*ii*) wall-mounted lamps and lanterns and old-fashioned street lamps, all using tungsten filament light bulbs
  (*iii*) uplighters and downlighters on standard poles up to 2.1 m (7 ft)
  (*iv*) spotlighting mounted on walls, pergolas and arches
   (*v*) bulkhead lights fitted into walls and steps.

It is vital to use only those fittings which are designed for outdoor, all-weather use. Some of these run on low voltage (for economy and safety), coupled with low wattage bulbs. In many cases, the area lit is quite small and so several fittings will be needed, especially alongside paths, driveways and even woodland walks. It does, however, ensure that only selected places are lit and not the whole garden, which creates more of an atmosphere than floodlighting, especially around patios and barbecues.

Coloured lighting

This can be high or low wattage/voltage. Coloured lighting should be used in a completely different way to white light. Its main use is in the lighting of plants, so low-level spotlights are often the most suitable type of fitting. The secret of success is not to try and create a daytime garden but one of fantasy. Many plants can take on a totally different appearance once coloured lighting is used on them. Here are some examples of which colours are particularly effective on certain plants:

GREEN LIGHT   used on yellow or pale green foliage, e.g. yellow variegated *Phormium*; variegated grasses and bamboo; *Lonicera nitida* 'Baggesons Gold'; *Choisya* 'Sundance'.

BLUE LIGHT   used on silver or grey foliage and white flowers, e.g. *Centaurea gymnocarpa*; *Santolina chamaecyparissus*; white petunias.

YELLOW LIGHT   used on green or yellow foliage, e.g. many conifers (use more powerful lighting here); grasses; bamboos in and around garden ponds.

RED LIGHT   generally poor on anything green but can be useful on some grey, silver or white plants.

ORANGE LIGHT   again, poor on green but quite effective on variegated or golden-leaved plants and on silver.

Coloured lighting can make quite large trees look very effective at night but needs to be powerful – perhaps 500 watts with good strong colour.

Index